COCKER SPANIELS

TODAY

JOYCE CADDY

RINGPRESS

Published by Ringpress Books Ltd,
POBox 8, Lydney, Gloucestershire GL15 6YD

Discounts available for bulk orders
Contact the Special Sales Manager at
the above address. Telephone 01594 563800

First Published 1995
© 1995 RINGPRESS BOOKS AND JOYCE CADDY

ISBN 1 86054 060 0

Printed and bound in Singapore
by Kyodo Printing Co

CONTENTS

4

FOREWORD

When I was invited to write this book – *Cocker Spaniels Today* – the title suggested that it should be a book about the breed as it is today, and how it has developed during the last twenty-five years or so. For this reason, I have deliberately not gone into the history of the breed in great depth. For anyone seeking to learn more about this, many other authors have covered the subject in depth.

During the last twenty-five years there have been considerable changes in the type of kennelling used, bedding, feeding methods, show ring presentation and even veterinary problems and treatments, as will be seen through the pages of this book.

However, one thing has not changed and that is the popularity of the delightful little dog, the Cocker Spaniel. For most people who have once owned a Cocker, no other breed will do. With his out-going temperament, the affection he shows to his owners, (and expects from them!), he is still one of the most popular breeds around. I hope this book will interest those who are thinking of having a Cocker, as well as to those who already own one or more, whether they be pets, working companions or show dogs.

JOYCE CADDY

ACKNOWLEDGEMENTS

My thanks are due to Sally Head for her art work to illustrate my interpretation of the Breed Standard; to Sue Rose for help with details of Field Trials, Tracking and Working Tests for Cockers in the USA; to my veterinary surgeon, Mr Brian Esplen, B.Vet.Med., MRCVS, of Minehead, for his help and advice when "vetting" the chapter on Health; to the Kennel Club for their help and co-operation; to Ian Scott for help in finding photographs of about twenty years ago which I did not have; to Kate Romanski, Marie-Louise Doppelreiter, Haja Van Wessem, Anja Puumala, Fran Minaar, Barbara Killworth, Herbert Klemann and Thomas Jakkel, for their help in writing about the Cocker scene in their own countries, and to all the owners from many countries who supplied photographs of their dogs.

INTRODUCTION

When we were first married, in the 1950s, we considered buying a Bulldog. Then we thought of a golden Cocker. In the Midlands, where we lived at the time, the obvious place to buy a golden puppy was the Lochranza kennels at Lichfield. They did not have one available, but they did have Jeremie, a sixteen-week-old blue roan and tan dog puppy. We fell in love with him and bought him.

Jeremie was purely our pet dog, but we were told by the breeders that they hoped we would show him at local shows. By six months, and with our interpretation of a book on the breed, we thought he would be almost unbeatable – he was to us! At his first show, he lay on his back for the judge to tickle his tummy. At the next show, we were told that he was very good, and we believed it. However, we soon came to realise that, though Jeremie enjoyed shows and so did we, he was not really good enough to win well. Cockers and shows had got us hooked, though, and we bought a black bitch, Bonny, who had won very well. We soon realised that a bitch in season, together with a dog in the house, did not make for a quiet life, so Jeremie had to spend a short holiday with my vet friend.

You live and learn. With Bonny we learned how easy it is to get a Cocker too fat. When we went abroad on holiday, she spent her time (Jeremie too) with my in-laws. Normal food, plus three family meals a day, are not exactly conducive to maintaining a trim figure, so drastic dieting for Bonny had to follow.

We took both dogs to Cornwall on holiday and showed them during our stay. We all enjoyed time on the beach – sadly you cannot take dogs on the beach during the summer months nowadays. Shortly after our return, Bonny developed hardpad (a form of distemper for which there were no inoculations at that time). This gave me a lesson in looking after a very sick bitch, and, fortunately, she recovered fully. We later mated her, but she had no puppies on that occasion. That taught me how to overcome disappointment. We then bought Merry, a black and white bitch puppy from Mr Lloyd's 'of Ware' kennels. She was later to become the foundation of our own kennels. Apart from Jeremie, we only kept bitches at that time. As Bonny did not have a bitch puppy, we kept nothing from her and concentrated on particolours, which we have done ever since. But the pleasure those dogs gave us more than made up for the things that went wrong.

They confirmed our opinion that the Cocker Spaniel is a most appealing breed and makes an ideal companion. Many people think that they have sad expressions, but they are actually happy, outgoing characters, whose sad, pleading expression can be turned on just to gain attention! If you are feeling happy, they will bustle around the place exuding pleasure too. Their expression at such times can be changed to one of almost a smile, eyes twinkling with fun.

Cockers are a hardy and adaptable breed, who can enjoy life in the country and be equally happy in a suburban situation. They are not really suitable dogs for a tower-block apartment life, as they need rather more exercise than can be provided in such surroundings.

They are active dogs, and like to be kept busy – if only chasing balls, or hunting rabbits in the hedgerows. They love old people and children alike, and quickly become established as a member of the family. They accept life at face value, and love getting attention, being groomed, taken for a walk, taken out in the car, and are generally easy to feed. They do tend to be rather greedy, and, like Oliver Twist, will always ask for more; and if overfed they do tend to put on weight, especially if they do not get a great deal of exercise.

Cockers are very intelligent dogs, and can be taught to do most tasks, e.g. as a gundog, in Obedience, Agility, etc., and they are quick to learn and eager to please. They do need time spent on regular grooming. Some grow quite profuse coats, especially some of the blacks and dark blue roans, but if this is dealt with regularly, it is quite easy to keep under control. They shed hair and, if not groomed, the coat will become tangled and difficult to deal with.

The lifespan of an average, well-cared-for Cocker is about twelve to fourteen years, though some do go on for longer than that. I have had three who lived to around the sixteen-year mark, and I recently heard of two litter brothers, brought up together, who died only a few weeks apart at the age of seventeen years.

Obviously, we are devoted to Cockers. They have given us great pleasure, both at home and in the show ring. They enjoy shows as much as we do, and it does not seem to matter to them if they win or lose. We have learned that, although we hope to gain top honours, there are lots of other Cocker exhibitors who have nice, happy dogs and who can reasonably expect their dogs to win too. Nothing can take away the feeling of elation at a big win. We will never forget the thrill of Ringo being Second Best of All Breeds at Crufts. Yes, and the memory of Ringo getting off the lead as we came out of Olympia following that win. Fortunately, he liked the look of a nearby telephone box on which to lift his leg – and I was able to put the lead back on! Also unforgettable is the thrill of a Best in Show win when he was ten and a half years old and had won a Veteran Class, while our current Champion had been beaten in the Breed classes.

Another thing I learned from Ringo was the great enjoyment a Cocker derives from doing the job he was originally bred for – working as a gundog. When I first became involved with the Show Spaniels Field Day at Loynton Hall (about five miles from where I lived), my first Show Champion would not pick up feather, and with few rabbits or hares around, did not retrieve well enough to run for his Qualifying Certificate.

With Ringo, however, I was fortunate that the land surrounding our property consisted

Ouaine Vivid Fairy Of Ware (1952-1964): The first particoloured bitch owned by Joyce Caddy, and the foundation bitch of the Ouaine Cockers.

of a large private 'shoot'. The gamekeeper, George Clarke (the father of George Clarke of Reulemill English Springer note, just a young boy when I first knew him but now a Championship Show judge of his breed), was extremely helpful, and taught me how to train Ringo. He provided a moorhen, which is a very tight-feathered bird, to introduce Ringo to feather, and also allowed me to use his land, with its abundant pheasants, for training purposes in between shooting days. I was perhaps lucky, in that Ringo very quickly proved to be a capable worker, and actually enjoyed going out on fourteen shooting days (nine driven game and five rough shoot) in the six-week training period before running for his Qualifying Certificate. During those six weeks, he also won the

Gundog Group at the Ladies' Kennel Association (LKA) Championship Show. After 'Qualifying' we were really thrilled, but his coat was beginning to suffer, so we withdrew him from shooting days.

I next took along a bitch, Gem, who proved to be a very good worker, and enjoyed it so much I worked her to the end of the season. She also won her Qualifying Certificate. Even years later, at about eleven, when her eyesight had failed from glaucoma in one eye and a dislocated lens in the other, she still loved to sit while I dragged a pheasant along the ground. She used her nose to follow the scent when I told her to 'find' it, and brought the bird back so proudly. She really loved doing this as a party-piece for any visitors we had. To help her get around the place and avoid bumping into rock walls, we gave her a slipper to carry, as a sort of radar or buffer. She loved that too.

As I write, memories come flooding back of high days and holidays, some sad days too, but nothing will let us forget Jeremie, Bonny, Merry, Gem, Ringo and all the others who have lived with us, and brought us so much pleasure with their friendly and happy-go-lucky natures. Their devotion to us has led us to the present time. We are fortunate enough to have plenty of space, and a field in which to exercise our dogs and play with them, developing their characters and enjoying their company at home, as well as at shows.

Little did I think when we first bought Jeremie that Cockers would become so much a part of my life. I have a great deal to thank them for. Because of Cockers, I have met many very interesting people from all over the world, and been to many countries which I would never have visited, had I not had the privilege of judging there. I have made so many friends through Cockers – both in the UK and overseas – all of whom share my love of the breed, and my opinion that Cockers make devoted companions and deserve to receive as much love and affection as they themselves offer.

Chapter One

A BROAD HISTORY OF THE COCKER SPANIEL

Many written references to Spaniels exist, dating back seven or eight hundred years. The indications are that they came originally from Spain as the Roman Empire expanded. There are also pictures which include Spaniel-type dogs, but it was in the latter half of the 19th century that the different Spaniel breeds as we know them began to evolve.

EARLY YEARS OF THE BREED

The first Kennel Club Stud Book (of which I am proud to own a copy) was issued in 1873, and gave details of dog shows since they were first held in 1859. At the second show, the prize list showed a class for "Cockers or other breeds" (with F. Burdett as the winner of the first prize), but it has the note: "Name of dogs unknown". This original stud book listed the dogs of each breed, but one section was Spaniels (Field, Cocker and Sussex). Very few entries showed to which of the breeds the dog belonged. One that did was:

"FLASH: Mr E. Sinnott's, Brislington, Bristol (Cocker).
            Born, 1870; Colour, liver and white;
            Shown by Mr J. Bishop and Mr S. Johnson;
            Pedigree, by Dash out of Flo;
            Chief performance, Crystal Palace; Extra prize, 1872."

In the early 1950s, a monthly magazine called The Cocker Spaniel Journal was produced. One issue included extracts from the Kennel Gazette and Kennel Review of the 1880s, including the following passage:

"'And licks his fingers though no meat be by
The generous Spaniel loves his masters eye'.
from On Man's Gratitude by Francis Quarles

"The Spaniel, it will be seen by the above lines, was chosen above all other dogs, more than 250 years ago (around 1630), for his generous and grateful nature, as an example to mankind, and to the present time these good qualifications have not degenerated, for he stands out boldly, the most useful, grateful and companionable to mankind. Nature was generous in giving such a creature to man, for him to form and cultivate into such a beautiful and useful animal.

"He is small yet large, in symmetry perfection; head beautifully moulded and beaming with intelligence; neck muscular for retrieving and body well balanced on short, straight and strong legs. He can be easily and highly trained and beside his own work of finding and flushing all kinds of game in the thickest covers, or in the open fields, he is equal to the Retriever on land or water, and can fill the gap of a Setter or Pointer with credit."

The writer did, however, go on to say: "Of Cockers proper there are but few. Many we see in the Cocker class are weeds, and wastrels of larger breeds.....with the exception of Little Dan, there has not been a dog shown, this year, that has any right to the name of Cocker. The liver and tan Jingo is a deformed wastrel. At the Palace show in January he with two others formed the worst class we ever saw."

The one exception, Little Dan, was owned by Richard Lloyd, founder of the Ware Kennels, and grandfather of the present prefix owner, Jennifer Carey.

The one really interesting dog of those years was Ch. Obo, born in June, 1879. At that time, dogs weighing over 25 lbs were classified as Field Spaniels. Those under 25 lbs were Cocker Spaniels. Obo came into the latter category, and it is generally agreed that all modern Cockers throughout the world can be traced back to him. His measurements, however, bear little relationship to the modern version of the breed:

Weight: 22 lbs
Height: 10 inches
Length from nose to eyes: two and a half inches
Length from nose to occiput: seven and a quarter inches
Length from nose to set on of tail: 29 inches.

The Cocker was recognised as a separate breed in 1892, but weighing continued until 1901, when the weight limit was abolished. The Cocker Spaniel Club was formed in 1902, and quickly established the first Breed Standard, which remained unchanged for almost fifty years and is reproduced below.

ORIGINAL STANDARD AND SCALE OF POINTS FOR JUDGING
Descriptive standard of the Cocker Spaniel
HEAD: A nicely-developed square muzzle and jaw; with distinct stop. Skull and forehead should be well developed, with plenty of room for brain power, cleanly chiselled and not cheeky.

EYES: Full but not prominent, hazel or brown coloured, harmonising with colour of coat, with a general expression of intelligence and gentleness, decidedly wide-awake, bright and merry.

EARS: Lobular, set on low, leather fine and not extending beyond the nose, well clothed with long silky hair, which should be straight – no positive curls or ringlets.

Exquisite Model Of Ware: Best in Show Crufts 1938 and 1939, winner of 53 CCs. Owned by Mr H.S. Lloyd.

Lucky Star Of Ware: Twice Best in Show at Crufts, winner of 39 CCs. Owned by Mr H.S. Lloyd.

NECK: Long, strong and muscular, and neatly set on to fine sloping shoulders.

BODY (including Size and Symmetry): Compact and firmly knit together, giving the impression of a concentration of power and untiring activity; the total weight should be about 25 to 28 lbs.

NOSE: Sufficiently wide and well developed to insure the exquisite scenting power of this breed.

SHOULDERS AND CHEST: The former sloping and fine, chest deep and well developed, but not too wide and round to interfere with the free action of the forelegs.

BACK AND LOIN: Short in back. Immensely strong and compact in proportion to the size and weight of the dog; slightly drooping towards the tail.

HINDQUARTERS: Wide, well rounded, and very muscular.

STERN: That most characteristic of blue blood in all the Spaniel family may, in the lighter and more active Cocker, although set low down, be allowed a slighter higher carriage than in the other breeds, but never cocked up over, but rather in a line with the back, although the lower the carriage and action the better, and when at work its action should be incessant in this, the brightest and merriest of the whole Spaniel family. Not docked too short.

FEET AND LEGS:The legs must be well boned, feathered and straight, for the tremendous exertions expected from this grand little sporting dog, and should be sufficiently short for concentrated power, but not too short as to interfere with its full activity. Feet firm, round and catlike, not too large or spreading or loose-jointed.

COAT: Flat and silky in texture, never wiry nor wavy, with sufficient feather, but not too profuse and never curly.

COLOUR: Various; in self-colours a white shirt frill should never disqualify, but white feet should not be allowed in any specimen of self-colour.

GENERAL APPEARANCE: That of an active, merry sporting dog. The Cocker Spaniel does not follow on the lines of the larger Field Spaniel, either in lengthiness, lowness or otherwise, but is shorter in back, and rather higher on the legs.

SCALE OF POINTS FOR JUDGING COCKER SPANIELS
Positive points

Head and Jaws	10
Eyes	5
Ears	5
Neck	10
Body	20
Fore-legs	10
Hind-legs	10
Feet	10
Stern	10
Coat and Feather	10
Total :	100

Negative points

Light Eyes	10
Light Nose	15

Hair curled on Ears (very undesirable)	15
Coat (curly, woolly, or wiry)	20
Carriage of Stern	20
Top Knot	20

Total Negative Points 100

Apart from height, then not included, and weight, which was increased to 28-32 lbs in the late 1960s, there is little difference in meaning from the current Breed Standard. The Kennel Club Breed Standard does not now include faults as in the past, but indicates that if the dog does not comply with the Standard in any way, then it should be regarded as a fault in proportion to its degree.

DEVELOPMENT OF THE COCKER
An article written in 1951 by Mr H. S. Lloyd, son of Richard Lloyd mentioned earlier, summed up the development of the breed from 1909 to the end of the Second World War.

1910	11 Championship Shows	22 Challenge Certificates
1920	31 Championship Shows	42 Challenge Certificates
1929	24 Championship Shows	48 Challenge Certificates
1939(War)	16 Championship Shows	32 Challenge Certificates
1949	28 Championship Shows	56 Challenge Certificates

He commented that hardly any of the 1910 dogs would win much at 1950s shows. The 1920s saw dogs that were heavy for their height, with great barrel ribs, ample bone and deep in brisket. Their heads were not as good as the 1950s dogs, but were sturdier. There was great improvement in the 1930s, and the outstanding Best in Show wins at Crufts of Lucky Star of Ware, and Exquisite Model of Ware, showed how well Cockers compared with other breeds. The Ware dogs of Mr Lloyd were easily the outstanding winners of the later inter-war years. The blue roan Lucky Star of Ware was Best in Show All Breeds at Crufts in 1930 and 1931. Exquisite Model of Ware, a black, white and tan bitch, was Best in Show at the Kennel Club and Crufts Show in 1938, and at Crufts in 1939. Whoopee of Ware, a blue roan dog, won 54 Challenge Certificates. In 1939, Exquisite Model won fourteen out of the sixteen Bitch CCs on offer that year.

In late 1939, Championship shows were abandoned because of the war, and it was not until 1946 that they were resumed. The Cocker Spaniel Club held the first. The Dog CC was won by Mr Lloyd with Hyperion of Ware, and Mrs Jamieson Higgins, famous for her Falconers Cockers, awarded the Bitch CC to Harmac Hycilla. Mr Lloyd continued to be very prominent and again showed a blue roan bitch, called Tracey Witch of Ware, to the top spot at Crufts twice.

WINNING DOGS AND OWNERS
New faces at the top were appearing, however. In particolours, Mr Collins with

Sh. Ch. Tracey Witch Of Ware: Twice Best in Show at Crufts, and once Best Bitch in Show Crufts. Owned By Mr H.S. Lloyd.

Ch. Colinwood Silver Lariot: Record Dog CC holder, with owner Mr A. Collins and judge Mrs J. de Casembroot (Treetops).

Colinwood, Mrs Gold with Oxshott (both solids and particolours), and Joe Braddon with of Ide were prominent, while Mrs Doxford (Broomleaf), Mrs Lucas-Lucas (Sixshot), Mrs de Casembroot (Treetops), and Miss Macmillan (Lochranza) were also among the leading exhibitors.

It seemed unlikely that the record number of CCs won would be surpassed, but this was achieved in the late 1950s and early 60s by Ch. Colinwood Silver Lariot (59 CCs), owned by Mr Collins. Even that record was later to be broken by Ch. Bournehouse Starshine, owned by Gordon Williams (who later had a Best in Show award at Crufts with his English Setter, Bournehouse Dancing Master). No subsequent dog has neared her total of 60 CCs, though both Sh. Ch. Cilleine Echelon, and my own Int. Ch. Ouaine Chieftain (both blue roan) passed the 30 CC mark. Cockers nowadays appear to develop earlier, but not to last as long in the show ring as they did in the past. Maybe this has something to do with modern coats and coat presentation.

Miss Macmillan's Sh. Ch. Lochranza Strollaway and my own Int. Ch. Ouaine Chieftain both achieved the Reserve Best in Show All Breeds spot at Crufts.

COCKERS TODAY

The personalities in the ring have changed over the last twenty-five years. Some of them have passed away – Jimmy Auld (Glencora), Arthur Mansfield (Lucklena), George Dunn (Merrybray), and Dorothy Hahn (Misbourne). Some of the other highly successful exhibitors in their day, such as Miss Macmillan (Lochranza), Pam Trotman (Kavora), Ron and Tydfil Bebb (Ronfil), and Phyllis Woolf (daughter of the late Mr Collins) and her husband Peter (Colinwood), do not show very often, although they are seen and welcomed at shows. Leslie Page is a top all-round judge, but has no Cockers nowadays. There are many more, and newcomers would do well to seek advice from these very knowledgeable old stagers.

One other thing which changed was the Kennel Club's introduction of the title of Show Champion in 1958. Up until that time, no matter how many CCs a gundog won, it could not be called a Champion until it had obtained a Qualifying Certificate by proving its worth in the field. From 1958 onwards, any gundog winning three CCs under three different judges was entitled to be described as a Show Champion, but, for the title of Champion, the Qualifying Certificate still needs to be gained. The Show Champion title was ruled to be retrospective, so that dogs which had won the necessary three CCs in former years could use the title.

In the past, the bigger kennels tended to have better results in the show ring, whereas nowadays the top Cocker wins tend to be spread more widely. In solids, Penny Lester has continued to stay at the top with the Quettadene dogs – a prefix successfully started by the late Mrs Woodbridge. As I write, Sh. Ch. Quettadene Mystique, a black bitch, is currently holding the No.1 position in the breed, and Penny has won well with other Cockers.

Ann and Alan Webster (Asquanne) have also been successful with both blacks and reds, and their Sh. Ch. Gonzales, a black dog, is proving to be an outstanding sire. Poppy Becker has continued with the Broomleaf line, as well as with her winning Olanzas, and the Kettle sisters must have had the thrill of their lives when Lujesa Fiore Dorato won the CC at Crufts in 1993, later achieving her Sh. Ch. title.

Top names in particolours at present must include Moray Armstrong with his Bitcons. He had won very well with bitches, but Sh. Ch. Bitcon Pacific Blue and Sh. Ch. Bitcon Troubador have shown how successful he can be with dogs.

Another kennel very much to the fore is Lynwater, owned by Elizabeth Maclean in Scotland. Her Sh. Ch. Lynwater Dawn Shimmer won the Gundog Group at Crufts in 1994, and her kennel manager, David Todd, must have been very pleased when the Cocker he had exported, Chataway Craftsman, was Best of Breed at the World Show in Switzerland in 1994. Many of the photographs in this book are of dogs which have been successful in the ring, and the owners are among the many who have achieved success at the top. The success of so many people does tend to show that for dedicated owners, who are prepared to be selective in their breeding, to rear and exercise their dogs properly, and to present them at their best in the ring, getting to the top is an achievable objective.

Chapter Two

THE COCKER SPANIEL PUPPY

The choice of a puppy is very important, whether it is destined to be a pet, a working dog, or a show dog. Equally important is the source from which the puppy is to be obtained. Unfortunately, there are quite a number of what are commonly called 'puppy farms' around the country, which breed and sell the commercially viable breeds, including Cockers. Many other dog dealers buy in puppies from various sources. My advice would be to avoid such establishments completely, and obtain a puppy from a private breeder. The secretaries of any of the Breed Clubs will always be happy to pass on details of club members who have puppies available.

COLOUR

The choice of colour is a matter of personal preference, and before making a decision, it would be wise for a prospective first-time Cocker owner to go to a Breed Club Show, or a Championship Show, and look at the dogs to decide which colour appeals most. A word of warning here, however, because some of the colours are not as numerous as others. For instance, orange and white, orange roan, black white and tan, and liver/chocolate roan are not nearly as numerous as blue roan; so if one of these colours is preferred, it may be necessary to wait a while to obtain one.

DOG OR BITCH

The next decision, again a very important one, is whether to have a dog or a bitch. I am often asked which I advise, and my reply is always that it depends on several factors. For example, if the puppy will be living in an area where local canine 'Romeos' are allowed to run free, a bitch who cannot be kept confined in a dog-proof garden while she is in season (every six-to-eight months or so), can create something of a problem. On the other hand, if she has to be taken out for a walk (beware of local dogs following!), a Cocker is small enough to carry for the first 50 yards or so from home, and the last 50 yards on the return journey, thus causing any following dogs to lose the scent. If there are small children in the house, who may accidentally leave the doors open when a bitch is in season, free-roaming dogs can be a nuisance, but this is a matter of care and observation on the part of the owner.

As far as sweetness of character is concerned, I have always found dogs to be just as

Cocker Spaniel puppies are always appealing, but you must not let your heart rule your head when it comes to choosing a puppy.

Photo courtesy: Miss M.L. Doppelreiter.

Colour is a matter of personal preference, but you may have to wait longer for your puppy if you opt for a colour such as orange and white, which is less numerous.

good as bitches. In some of the larger, guarding breeds, males can be much more 'macho' than females, but I have not found this to be so with Cockers. A dog puppy at five-to-six months of age can be a bit more independent than a bitch, and when called, may delay slightly before coming, and when he does he may look at his owner as if to say: "You didn't really want me before, did you?" But a little bit of bribery, with a reward when he obeys, will work wonders, and set good habits.

SHOW PUPPIES
If a puppy is to be for show, it should be made clear to the breeder exactly what is required. No-one should expect a puppy bought strictly as a pet to be a top show winner: if one does turn out to be so, then the new owner is indeed very fortunate. It may not be possible to obtain a 'pick-of-the-litter' puppy immediately, as many breeders will wish to keep one for themselves, but good things are worth waiting for, so you should allow time

to find the ideal puppy. However, it should be emphasised that, no matter how promising a puppy of eight-to-ten weeks may look, no-one can guarantee that it will reach any given standard. The most one can say is that, if it goes on as it is at that age, the puppy has the potential to be a show dog. Many things affect the development of a puppy as it grows – not least is the rearing – so, unless it stays with the breeder, no promise can or should be made.

If the puppy is destined for the show ring, any beginner to showing would be wise to ask an experienced person to help with the choice. Experienced breeders have a personal preference for the age at which they like to choose their puppies, and for me, eight weeks is the ideal time. At that age, I feel that they are miniatures of what they will be at eight months. They may go through various less attractive stages in between, but by eight months, if all has gone well, they will be grown-up versions of the eight-week stage, and will just need time to develop and mature. If the choice was correct, who knows what success may follow?

ASSESSING SHOW PUPPIES

At eight weeks, I like to see good bone; small, tight feet; straight front legs (no loose elbows); and a short, deep, well-ribbed body. The hindquarters should show good width of thigh and a nice bend of stifle, even at this early age. The hocks should not turn in or out, and the lower leg below the hock should be relatively short. The head should have a nicely-balanced muzzle and skull, with good stop, and good width of nostril and foreface, and the neck should lead into fine sloping shoulders. The eyes should have tight rims, and a sweet expresson. The ears should be set on level with the eyes, but it must be remembered that an alert puppy often carries its ears a bit high, even though they are correctly set.

The tail set is also important, as puppies do sometimes carry their tails a bit too high. If the set-on of tail is correct, it should be carried correctly when the puppy is older, but if the set-on is too high, the tail will usually not be carried correctly, even when older.

An eight-week-old tricolour male: In Cocker Spaniels, the males are just as sweet-tempered as the females.

Photo courtesy: Miss M.L. Doppelreiter.

It is helpful if you can see the litter with their mother, as this will give you an idea of how the puppies are likely to develop.

If the mouth at eight weeks shows a correct bite, it does not guarantee that it will be correct at the change of teeth at about four months, as occasionally the second teeth may come through incorrectly – though teeth which are correct at eight weeks usually stay that way. But do not expect an incorrect bite at eight weeks to right itself at four months, though it is just possible that it may.

Unless the puppy can be seen moving steadily, for example in the garden, it is difficult to assess movement. However, if the puppy is constructed properly, it should move well.

Temperament is very important – a timid puppy will rarely make a bold, outgoing show dog. A happy, tail-wagging puppy has much more chance of success.

CHOICE OF WORKING DOGS

If a puppy is required purely for working as a gundog, and its future working ability is of more importance than its appearance as a show Cocker, a breeder of Field Trial Cockers would be able to provide such a puppy. The Cocker Spaniel Club has a Field Trial Section, and could put a prospective owner in touch with suitable breeders. If a Cocker with working ability (but not necessarily as fast as a Field Trial dog) is required, and you also want one which looks more like the show Cocker, the London Cocker Spaniel Society holds working tests and would be able to provide details of members who work their dogs. Many show-bred Cockers have the ability to work, if given the opportunity.

All the puppies I have had have been eager to carry things – balls, sticks, bones, etc. –

and when played with, will retrieve them. This instinct is always there, and can be built on as the puppy grows.

POINTS TO REMEMBER
No matter for what purpose you are buying the puppy, it should always be a bold, friendly, outgoing character. A shy, nervous puppy, however sympathetic one may feel towards it, is not a typical Cocker puppy. Eyes should be bright, not running or with sticky discharge, and noses should be moist with no discharge. The coat should be flat and silky, and the body should be firm and plump, but not too fat. The legs should be well-boned, and feet compact and tight.

PREPARING FOR YOUR PUPPY
Preparations for a new puppy should include:
a) Provision of a sleeping place – a basket or plastic bed, with suitable cosy bedding.
b) A water bowl – always have clean, fresh water available for the puppy to drink as he wishes.
c) A feeding bowl – the breeder will advise on which type the puppy is used to.
d) Lots of newspapers for the floor in case of 'accidents'.
e) Old towels for drying wet feet and legs in bad weather.
f) Food – the breeder will advise in advance of the type and quality. Speaking personally as a breeder, I always provide sufficient food of the type the puppy is accustomed to for a few days after he leaves my home. This avoids any upset tummies or bowels while he is being house-trained. All responsible breeders provide a feeding chart, or diet sheet, with advice on how to continue as the puppy grows. This should be kept handy and referred to frequently. If the new owner has any worries, however small, he should be encouraged to phone the breeder for advice.
g) A brush and comb.

ARRIVING HOME
If the puppy is to be a pet, remember that, during the first few days, he will probably miss his litter-mates. In order to help him to settle into the new surroundings, he should be made as comfortable as possible, and taken outside to relieve himself on arrival.

If there are small children in the house, they must be taught that the puppy needs to sleep quite a lot and should not be disturbed as and when they feel like it. Sometimes a puppy will cry when left alone at night in a new, strange, place. I have never used one, but I have been told that if a clock is well-wrapped in a towel or blanket, and placed in the puppy's bed, the sound of its ticking will simulate another puppy's heartbeat, and will help your solitary puppy to settle down.

Particularly if the weather is cold, a well-wrapped hot-water bottle can be placed in the puppy's bed – remember that he has been sleeping with other puppies and may miss their body warmth. Another tip which may help is to leave a small light on, such as a child's nightlight. Once the puppy is really at home in his new surroundings, this can be removed.

Bear in mind that your puppy will wish to relieve himself as soon as he wakes and that any sounds in the house like a toilet flushing, or a radio playing, will wake him. He should be taken out straightaway. He will not be able to wait for half an hour, until his new owner has showered and dressed! Putting on a housecoat or dressing gown and letting the puppy out is better than risking a dirty kitchen floor. As your pup gets older, he will learn to wait longer.

At such an early age, puppies do not understand a lot of words, so it is best to keep any commands simple. A sharp "No" when he is doing something he shouldn't, and "Good boy" in a gentler tone when he does something right, quickly become understood. But if you use "No" sometimes, then "Don't do that" or "Stop it" on other occasions, the puppy will become more and more confused. All the family should use the same commands, to help the puppy understand what is required of him.

How the puppy develops, not only physically, but as far as character and social behaviour are concerned, will be up to the new owner. Dogs are creatures of habit, and keeping to a routine will be of great help to both owner and puppy. Time and patience, with kindness and affection, will work well in raising a happy, well-behaved, socially-acceptable dog, who will be a pleasure to live with.

HOUSE TRAINING

If growing puppies are kept in the house (though by about eight weeks many breeders have transferred them to a kennel), house-training will be made easier if you remember that, on waking up and immediately after a meal, your puppy will want to relieve himself. If at other times he starts to move around in circles, this is another indication that he should be taken outside. If the owner is observant, training should be no problem. Don't blame the puppy if you take no notice of him and he slips up. Praise for your puppy when he obliges and performs outside will help him to realise that he has done the right thing.

Apart from cleanliness, house-training also covers the aspect of not allowing the puppy to chew things up (e.g. carpets, shoes, slippers etc.). When he is seen doing this, a firm "No" will tell him he is wrong.

Commands should always be simple, and the same command should be used each time by all members of the family. This will greatly help a puppy who is doing his best to please. The words "Good boy" or "Good dog" – whichever you prefer – should be used in a friendly tone, with much fussing and pleasure each time he does something good. He will quickly associate this with doing what you want of him. Tone of voice is all-important.

He should be taught to come when called. If he does not always respond quickly, try bribery, rather than let him get into bad habits (which are always difficult to break). Offering a reward will almost always work and does no harm, as it encourages him to come to you. When the response is swift and reliable, the rewards can be phased out gradually.

One other important thing is that all dogs should be taught to have their food dishes moved while they are eating, and that they must happily give up things like bones or balls to anyone. There should be no possessiveness. If they do not readily do this, they should

If you plan to show your Cocker Spaniel, you must be guided by the breeder, who will have assessed the puppies for their show potential.

TLC Photos.

A new puppy has a lot of new experiences to get used to when first arriving in a new home. It is important to give plenty of reassurance at this vulnerable time.

Photo courtesy: Miss M.L. Doppelreiter.

be encouraged to do so by means of bribery. There may be a time when the dog must give up something he has picked up (such as a dead bird which may be putrid), and he should not be allowed to refuse to give it up. For the experienced person it may be unnecessary to say that, in teaching a dog to give up his feeding bowl or playthings, he should never be teased unmercifully while being taught. For the novice, it is a point worth making.

Cocker puppies love to play with balls, and most will happily retrieve a ball rolled along the ground. Do not do this to excess, or your puppy may get bored with the game. House dogs usually have rather more chance of play, particularly on long, dark winter evenings, than kennel dogs, but they all appreciate a bit of fun with their owner. We taught my first Cocker the difference between a ball and a bone, a shoe and a slipper, and so on, – a lesson/game which he remembered till old age. He loved finding a hidden toy, always hidden within a reachable height for him. Fun for him, and for us!

BEDDING

Bedding for dogs should be washable so that it can be kept clean. Cockers, with their feathering, do tend to bring mud on dirty, wet days, and dust in dry weather, into the house, and bedding does get soiled. Wicker baskets are very nice to look at and comfortable for the dog, especially when a blanket is placed in the bottom. They do, however, have a tendency to unravel and come apart at the edges, if chewed up a bit. They are quite expensive nowadays, so I would not recommend one, at least until your puppy has overcome any chewing habits. Plastic beds, usually oval in shape, make an excellent alternative as they are virtually unchewable, draughtproof and can easily be washed out. They are not very cosy, though, so a piece of blanket or Vetbed should be used to provide more comfort. Many people find these ideal for indoor or kennel bedding.

At most Championship shows, or in larger pet stores, it is possible to buy other types of bedding such as duvets and bean-bags. Dogs find both very cosy and comfortable to lie on, but do not let a puppy chew a bean-bag – the result is small polystyrene beads all over the place! However, they make excellent bedding for an older dog, who may need a bit more warmth and softness than just a blanket in a plastic bed.

GROOMING

All puppies should be accustomed to being brushed and having their ears combed at an early age, and advice should be given to new owners on the way to do this. More details about grooming will be found elsewhere in this book, but I mention it here in relation to helping new owners to care for their puppies properly. Regular grooming is one aspect of that.

THE GROWING PUPPY

TEETHING

At about four months of age, puppies lose their baby teeth and the new adult teeth appear. Sometimes, during the teething process, a puppy's gums will become quite swollen and sore. At this stage, all hard food should be avoided. When the new teeth are through, a few biscuits will be welcomed. At this age the structure of the jaw and dentition should be checked again, as it does sometimes happen that things go wrong. For example, if the mouth is undershot, or the teeth out of line, a puppy should be discarded from showing or breeding plans. Most breeders regard what are loosely called bad mouths as a serious fault, and if allowed into a breeding programme they are extremely difficult to breed out. Such bad mouths are usually penalised quite heavily in the show ring too.

INOCULATION

All puppies should be inoculated, and advice from the veterinary surgeon should be followed, as such advice can vary depending on environment and area. Dogs in rural

Your puppy must be confined to the house and garden until the inoculation programme has been completed.

Photo courtesy: Miss M.L. Doppelreiter.

areas may only need to be inoculated once (usually two injections two weeks apart at about three months of age), but annual boosters are always recommended.

Puppies living in urban or city areas, where infectious and/or contagious diseases are more prevalent, are usually inoculated at three months of age (two injections two weeks apart) and again at twelve-monthly intervals.

Your own vet will be aware of the local situation, and will advise accordingly. My vet, Brian Esplen of Minehead, prefers to see a puppy as soon as it arrives at its new home, to check that it is healthy and free from infectious and contagious diseases, so that the puppy can be maintained in good health until ready for inoculation. (If your puppy is from a large breeding establishment or puppy farm, this is very good advice.)

However, I and many private kennel owners do not like the puppy to be taken to a surgery at an early age because of the risk of him picking up an infection. The safest possible way is for the vet to visit the home of the puppy. The next best thing would be for the owner to take the puppy to the surgery, but to leave it in the car, and ask the vet to come out and inspect (and even inoculate) the puppy there.

If none of these options is possible to arrange, the puppy should be carried carefully into the surgery (both owner and pup must avoid contact with any other dogs in the waiting room), and placed on its own blanket for examination.

Many vets work not only with daily surgeries, but also operate an appointment system. This may be a little more expensive, but is well worth it, as it avoids unnecessary risks from contact with other sick dogs in a waiting room.

SOCIALISATION AND SHOW TRAINING

All puppies need to be socialised to learn how to mix with people and other dogs. Naturally, this cannot be done until the inoculation process is over, but by that time the puppy will be coming up to four months of age. Many people find that taking puppies to a

Ringcraft training class does help to socialise them, even if the owner is not really interested in showing. If you do this when your puppy is so young, you must take great care to see that he is not frightened by bigger or more boisterous dogs. Any fright at this age can take a long time to get over.

Taking the puppy out from the house or kennel, around the garden, and maybe for a ride in the car, will get him used to different sights and sounds. Life should be made fun for puppies – though some of them regard going on a lead for the first time as anything but fun! It is useful to start lead training at home in the garden, and a good idea, if the lead is resented, is to take along with the puppy an older, steady dog on another lead. This will usually help. If your puppy still resents the lead around his neck, try putting on a small collar with lead attached, and let him run around with this trailing behind. He may try to chew the trailing lead, but will soon get used to the feeling of it being attached to him.

Teaching a puppy to stand for examination on a table, as in the show ring, can be done at home, before and after grooming. Once the puppy is used to this, other people should be asked to run their hands over him, to get him used to being handled on a table. This method can also apply to dogs which are not to be shown, but may at some stage of their lives have to be examined by a vet. Puppies usually take to this quite easily. If you go to training classes, you will practise this as part of the course.

Cockers are normally extrovert characters who accept new surroundings and new people without worrying. If too much training is done at a young age, some puppies may get rather bored with it all, and not show their happy character at its best – so try not to overdo it.

Chapter Three

ADULT CARE

As a breed, Cockers are easy to look after, and details regarding breeding, trimming, showing etc. will be found in the respective chapters. In general terms, the main things you can do to ensure a healthy, happy Cocker are:

1. Provide the best quality food you can afford, remembering always that dogs are meat-eating animals. Cockers need a fairly high-protein, rather than a high-carbohydrate diet, as they can put on weight easily, especially if they do not have a fair amount of exercise.
2. Make sure you do not overfeed, as Cockers can be quite greedy.
3. Provide comfortable sleeping quarters, whether the dog lives indoors or in an outside building or kennel.
4. Make sure that a young dog, or a dog who is getting on in years, gets plenty of rest and is not frequently disturbed, especially by children.

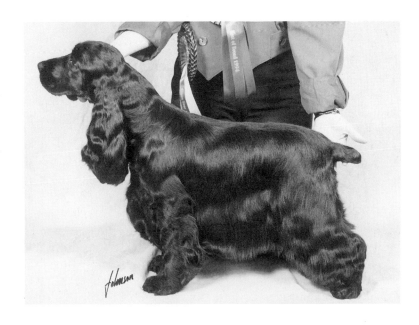

Irish Sh. Ch. Allies Second Edition: A beautifully groomed Cocker Spaniel with a gleaming coat.

Photo; Carol Ann Johnson.

*Misty at Dartmeet:
A well-trained
Cocker Spaniel is a
joy to be with.*

5. Groom the dog regularly, and bath when necessary.

6. Provide sufficient exercise and activity to prevent boredom.

7. Give training, so that you have an obedient dog who will be a joy to you, and never a nuisance to other people.

8. Be prepared to spend time with your dog, enjoy his company and let him enjoy yours, both giving and receiving affection and loyalty.

9. Last, but certainly not least, build up a good relationship with your vet and follow his advice regarding inoculations, and any treatment your dog happens to need.

MODERN KENNEL MANAGEMENT

Many people start off with one Cocker bitch, have a litter and keep a bitch puppy, and, with a daughter from that one kept a year or so later, find themselves in a comparatively short space of time with numbers building up rapidly. If numbers get too great to have all the dogs living in the house, you need to decide whether to use a kennel.

A dog kennel used to conjure up a picture of a box-like structure about three feet square in a small back yard! No doubt a few of those still exist, but modern breeders go for more space and air for their dogs.

Before setting up a kennel, the breeder must consider various points such as:

a) The financial aspect – how much can he afford?

b) How many dogs does he keep, or intend to keep?

c) Is the kennel merely to house dogs, or will it need to have a whelping kennel or a puppy kennel?

d) Where will the it be sited? How much space is available?

e) What materials will be used for its construction? Is it to be a portable building or a permanent one?

f) Thought must be given to the closeness to neighbours, and their attitude to dogs in general and to a number of dogs in particular.

g) What are the local council regulations about keeping a number of dogs?

Obviously personal preference will come into the decision in some respects, but a very wide range of portable kennels is available nowadays. Any breeder intending to set up a kennel would be well-advised to look at literature issued by various manufacturers before making any decision. It would also be useful to visit one or two local kennels to get an idea of what is possible and see which type would suit his needs best.

Permanent buildings of brick or stone construction can be very good, and will provide warmth in winter and be cool in summer. However, concrete block constructions can be rather cold and heating may be necessary in the winter months. Also, bear in mind that permanent buildings are usually more expensive to erect than portable ones.

Portable buildings constructed of timber are available in many shapes and sizes. They are usually warm and dry, but can be subject to damage by dogs who are destructive. They also require a little more maintenance than permanent buildings, needing to be waterproofed annually. Some manufacturers produce buildings made from plastic materials. These are very easy to keep clean, but rather expensive to buy.

Breeders who live in rural areas are often fortunate to have brick or stone outbuildings of the stable, loose-box or barn type, which can be made into excellent kennels. Urban dwellers do not have the opportunity of such structures, and may have to settle for portable timber buildings.

If only two or three dogs are to be kept, a strongly-constructed garden shed about eight feet by eight and at least six feet high can be adapted to suit. For more than that number, you will need a larger building so that the dogs have space to move around freely. All buildings should be light and airy, with windows or ventilation points on both sides to give good air circulation. The higher the building, the better for air circulation too.

A very useful building is the corridor-type kennel, which has pens down one side and a corridor down the other. This enables the owner to go into the kennel and attend to the dogs without having them all jumping up at the same time, and without getting wet himself in bad weather. Ideally, if space and finance allow, the building should have a space at one end where the dogs can play in really bad weather. This type of kennel with a number of pens also means that dogs and bitches can be separated if necessary, and so can boisterous puppies and old-age pensioners, who may need a bit more rest. Stable-type doors, where the top half can be opened while the lower part stays closed, are very useful, especially on hot days or nights, when windows and doors need to be open and yet dogs have to be kept in.

Whatever type of kennel is used, always bear in mind that space to exercise the dogs is extremely important. Here again, rural dwellers will be fortunate in ease of access to fields, woods, and open country, while town-dwellers may have to take the dogs to a local park or even just around the block.

Apart from regular exercise, space for the dogs to run freely close to the kennel is a great help. They can be let out to relieve themselves, which in turn helps to prevent fouling of the kennel building. Weldmesh, chain-link fencing, or the more modern sectional metal-framed mesh fencing are all very useful to make a compound for exercise.

For convenience, water and electricity should be laid to the kennel. If it is to have surface wiring, all electric cables and sockets must be overhead so that they cannot be disturbed by the dogs. As for water, fresh drinking water should be available at all times. Water bowls should be changed frequently, not just topped up, because it is surprising how much saliva from the dogs' mouths falls into the bottom of the bowl. Water should be changed at least twice a day, and more often in hot weather. If the dogs are allowed to stay out in the compound for any length of time, a bucket of water placed there is ideal. There is nothing worse on a cold winter's morning than having to carry water from the house – hence the suggestion that water be laid to the kennel.

Bedding can be of blankets or other fleecy fabrics. Some breeders choose to use straw in the winter, and others prefer shredded paper. All should be changed frequently, and beds kept clean. Beds can be of the plastic type which are easily washable, but in the winter I like to use wooden boxes with removable lids. These tend to keep the dog's body warmth inside the box and be warmer than open-topped beds, but in very cold weather when heating may be necessary, the lids can be removed and infra-red lamps placed over the boxes.

Newspapers may be used to cover the floors, but if these become wet with urine, they can be very smelly and difficult to dispose of. Many breeders use a thin layer of sawdust on the kennel floor. It is clean, very absorbent and prevents dogs from paddling around in urine or spilt water from drinking bowls. It is easily brushed out from the dogs' coats too. Disposal of soiled sawdust is frequently done by means of burning in a garden incinerator.

Whatever type of kennel you decide on, the dogs' welfare must always be the first consideration. Cramped, cold or damp conditions are not good for dogs. If the kennel is to house a number of dogs, it should ideally have a kennel kitchen and an isolation kennel for sick dogs, though most people prefer to bring a dog who is ill into the house to keep a close watch on it more easily.

FEEDING ROUTINE
Dogs in general, and Cockers in particular, are creatures of habit. They quickly become accustomed to being fed at a given time of day or evening, and you should establish a

routine and maintain it. Dogs get used to waiting their turn to be fed. Personally, I do not approve of feeding a number of dogs from one bowl or container, and always feed my dogs in separate bowls. This way they each have their own share – some more than others, depending on age or condition – and stick to their own bowls. Some dogs eat more quickly than others, so care should be taken to see that no dog gets his own share and part of someone else's. Cockers are rather greedy dogs and will, like Oliver Twist, ask for more. They will usually eat more than they really need, if allowed to do so.

As mentioned elsewhere, the type of feed given is a decision for the owner, but Cockers will eat almost any sort of food. Whatever type you use, it should always be freshly prepared, particularly in hot weather. A refrigerator and freezer are invaluable aids in the kennel kitchen. The fridge will keep food fresh, and quantities can be stored in the freezer until required, always allowing plenty of time for it to thaw out thoroughly before feeding. In all areas there are suppliers who will deliver foods in larger quantities, but you should take care not to store it for long periods. The fresher the better.

KENNEL COMPANIONS

Most Cockers are agreeable to their kennel companions – they should be so if they are typical Cocker Spaniels – but if there is any discord, it must be discouraged at a very early age. Some puppies play very roughly, but do not mistake this for aggression. Nor should you ever allow it to develop into aggression.

When dogs and bitches are kennelled together, watch out for bitches coming into season, and separate them until the season is over. A separate kennel, away from the one housing the dogs, is ideal.

CARE OF THE OLDER DOG

If a breeder is a genuine dog lover, he will keep his old dogs until the end of their days. They have no doubt given a great deal of pleasure during their earlier years, but when the time comes for retirement they should be allowed to live out their lives in comfort and happiness, in peaceful surroundings.

In winter, extra warmth may be necessary. In a kennel environment an infra-red lamp is appreciated, and it is easy to provide, inexpensive, and comfort-providing.

Care and attention to health or injury is important. Teeth sometimes need attention by the vet. If teeth have to be scaled, or removed, the mouth and gums may be a little sore for a few days, and soft food should be given until the 'oldie' can cope with normal food again.

Whatever happens, the old-faithfuls should never be tossed to one side – they will have given a great deal of affection and loyalty over many years and deserve consideration and care to the end. A caring owner should never keep more dogs than he can look after properly and can afford to feed and house in good conditions. He should also keep them true to type and character, so that all will be able to mix together harmoniously.

I well remember some years ago visiting Jean Smith's Sorbrook kennel and being impressed by seeing the dogs, of all ages from eight-week-old puppies to veterans, including stud dogs and bitches, all running together in the paddock on a fine day without

Finnish Ch. Astrawin Action Man, pictured at eleven years old. As your Cocker Spaniel advances in years, you must give extra consideration to the dog's general care and comfort.

any sign of disagreement or jealousy. A few cats were also wandering around happily too! Fortunately, my own dogs have always been a very agreeable lot, and youngsters and oldies get on well. I couldn't enjoy living with them, and they wouldn't be typical Cockers, if they didn't!

CARE OF THE COAT

A healthy Cocker should have a flat, silky-textured topcoat, with a denser undercoat. With the longer hair, or feathering, on the legs, body, and ears, quite a bit of dust, or mud on wet days, can be collected. When the dog is dry, this can usually be brushed out.

If the dog is out of condition, it will be reflected in the condition of the coat, which will lose its shine. Lack of attention to grooming will also have the same effect. The presence of internal parasites (worms) will create a dull coat, and a young puppy with worms will have a very tufty, patchy coat.

Care of the coat comes under the following headings:

1) Keeping the coat clean and in good condition.
2) Regular grooming.
3) Show trimming.

HYGIENE

Coats that are regularly brushed and combed will not get as dirty as those that are neglected. Bathing can remove much of the dirt, but not any tangles caused by neglect. Dogs, apart from show preparation, should only be bathed when necessary. Shampoos nowadays are such that the old idea of a bath removing the natural oils from a dog's coat is far from correct. Modern canine shampoos, like those for humans, have improved tremendously in recent years, and conditioners are also available. Take care to check that they do not contain colouring, which would be against Kennel Club regulations, if the bathing is being done as show preparation.

I prefer to use a separate shampoo and conditioner, although combined ones are available. The PH balance of the two is different, or so a Cocker exhibitor/hairdresser tells me! I do not know the technical details of this; I simply go by results.

EXTERNAL PARASITES

External parasites (fleas, lice etc.) are not nearly as common or difficult to deal with as they used to be. They can be treated with modern insecticidal shampoos if only a light infestation is present. If the dog is heavily infested, a vet will be able to advise on the type of treatment needed.

BATHING

My advice regarding bathing is to remember first of all to plug the dog's ears with cotton wool, to prevent water getting into the ear passages which are very deep. Remember to remove the earplugs when you have finished. It is easiest to stand the dog in the bath and, with the shower head held in one hand, wet him thoroughly all over with warm – not hot – water. When bathing, I always prefer to use running water, with the bath plug removed, so that I am using clean water all the time.

When bathing a dog with external parasites, particularly fleas, first wet and rub shampoo into the neck and throat area of the dog, to prevent the fleas moving up on to the head, where they are more difficult to deal with because of the risk of getting shampoo into the dog's eyes. This traps the fleas on the body where it is easier to use an insecticidal shampoo. There are many on the market, but always follow the instructions carefully.

For a normal bath, after wetting the dog, work in a good shampoo all over, lather well and rinse thoroughly. Shampoo again before giving another rinse, making sure the coat is squeaky-clean.

A good-quality conditioner can next be applied, allowed to stay in the coat for a few minutes, then rinsed out. A few drops of glycerine in the final rinse helps to enhance the shine on the coat. Prepare this before starting to bath the dog. Mix in a jug, and have it ready to pour over the dog after the last spray rinse. Then take a large towel and envelop the dog in it, or he will shake and splash water everywhere! Next, put him on a table, and rub all the surplus water out. The best way to finish drying – especially for a Cocker before a show – is to use a hair dryer. The dog quickly gets used to the noise and heat. If you are dealing with one dog, a hand-held hair dryer is fine, but for drying several dogs before a show, a stand dryer, which leaves both hands free, is much quicker.

Before switching on the dryer, a few preparations are useful. Take a fairly large towel, and fold one-third of it back to form a thicker part. Comb the dog through, and get all the hair lying flat in the direction of the natural growth of the coat.

Place the towel over the dog, with the thicker part over the neck and the single part over the rest of his back. Then take a 'nappy'-type safety pin and pin the towel edges together, drawing them tightly under the throat. Next, make sure it is tightly pulled down and pinned with a second safety pin under the dog's tummy, and another under the tail. This will hold the body coat flat, provided it was combed flat first, while the featherings and ears are dried.

The feathering on the back of the thighs should be blow-dried first, while brushing with a pin brush. If the dog has a very sensitive skin, a bristle brush should be used instead of a pin brush. When the feathering on the thighs is dry, the lower back legs and the feet should be dried. The front leg feathering should be dealt with next, in the same way. The hair under the front legs close to the body can be dried by holding each leg forward in turn and blowing warm air under the 'armpits'.

The chest feathering will be partly dry by now, so should be finished off by blow-drying and brushing all the feathering on the front of the chest as far as possible while the towel is still in place. The rest can be easily dried off when the towel is removed.

The next stage is dealing with the ears. Dogs are sometimes not too happy to have the noise of the dryer close to their ears, so check that the dog has not lost his earplugs. If he has, some more should be put in, before you start to blow-dry. Blow-drying and brushing at the same time will soon dry all the long hair on the ears.

By the time all this is done, the heat from the dryer will have partially dried the body coat, through the towel. The towel should then be removed, and the body coat blow-dried, blowing and brushing in a downwards direction to keep the coat flat.

Finally, give a little more attention to featherings, before checking that the dog is thoroughly dry, at which point the earplugs should be removed.

OTHER MEANS OF CLEANING THE COAT

DRY-CLEANING: For a quick clean-up of a coat when bathing is not suitable, as in the case of a sick dog, a very old dog in cold weather, or a bitch in season when it is best left till the season is over, there are preparations available for dry-cleaning the coat. These usually consist of a very fine powder and spirit in an aerosol container. They can be sprayed into the coat, then left to dry for a few minutes, before being brushed out. Take great care to avoid the dog's eyes if you use such preparations.

FOAM SHAMPOOS: These are also in aerosol containers, and are sprayed on and rubbed into the coat, and then towelled off. The whole coat can be dealt with, without getting the dog really wet.

CHALK POWDER: This also helps to clean the coat of a dog with a lot of white in it, but it is a rather dusty process, and needs to be done out-of-doors. The powder must also be thoroughly removed before going into the show ring, or it would contravene Kennel Club regulations.

GENERAL GROOMING

The reason for general grooming is to keep the coat tidy, with a nice appearance and as near as possible to the Standard requirements. Regular grooming, by brushing out the body and featherings well, followed by a fine comb on the body, or a wide-toothed comb on the featherings, will remove a lot of loose hair and prevent tangles forming. It will also keep the dog generally tidy, and at the same time reduce the number of hairs shed around the house or kennel.

From time to time, you will need to trim your dog's feet by removing with scissors all the surplus hair from the tops and sides of the feet, and underneath them, but never between the pads.

Grooming should be a time of enjoyment for the dog, with praise and maybe a reward when he is well-behaved. A dog unused to regular grooming may resent it to start with, and you will need to be firm, but kind. Even with a young puppy, although he will not need as much grooming as when he is older, the procedure should be done regularly so that he gets used to it. Dogs, being very much creatures of habit, quickly get used to being given attention, and grow to enjoy being groomed.

Novice pet owners should be warned that, if they do not feel able to trim their dog themselves and decide to take it to a beauty parlour, the trimming will most likely be done in the form of clipping, leaving the dog quite heavily shorn. It is much better to ask the dog's breeder to recommend someone in the area who will trim the dog and leave it looking like a Cocker, even if they do not do a complete show trim. Always remember that a well-groomed dog is much easier to trim. If the breeder cannot recommend anyone, the secretary of the nearest Breed Club will be able to help.

SHOW TRIMMING

This takes grooming a step or so further, but if the general grooming above is done on a regular basis, it makes show trimming so much easier. For anyone new to show trimming, it would be a good idea to go to a show, look closely at the top winning dogs and see how they are presented. Remember that the objective of show trimming is to make your dog look as good as possible, and convince the judge that he is the best one there. Careful trimming will show up a dog's good points, and hide the bad ones. The judge has only a very short time to look at each dog, and first impressions are most important.

There are many types and sizes of grooming tools available on the market. Whichever type you decide upon, choose something which is comfortable for your own use.

The basic tools needed are a slicker brush to remove tangles; a wide-toothed comb; a fine-toothed comb (Spratts 76 without a handle, or 73 with a handle); a bristle brush; thinning scissors and straight-bladed scissors; a rubber glove and your own finger and thumb!

SHOW TRIMMING
Photography Carol Ann Johnson.

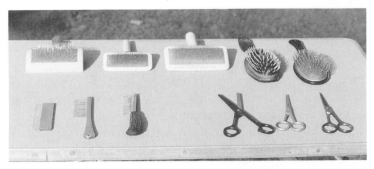

Grooming tools: Buy good-quality tools, and they will last a long time.

Trimming is easier if the dog stands on a table, on a non-slip rubber mat.

A Cocker will have a rough coat if it has not been trimmed for some time, and you will need to use a wide-toothed comb to remove the loose hair.

If you look after them, the tools will last for a long time, so buy the best quality you can afford. It will be well worth it in the long run. Try not to let the scissors fall to the floor, as the points can easily be damaged. If scissors are used on a dirty coat, they will quickly become blunt.

Trimming is made easier if the dog is put on a table which is of a convenient height to avoid backache for the person doing the trimming, and small enough to prevent the dog pulling away, yet large enough for the dog to stand comfortably and maybe lie down flat. The table should be fairly solid, not lightweight and rocky. There are purpose-made tables with a non-slip surface obtainable nowadays, but if you do not have one, a kitchen table or bench, covered with a piece of heavy rubber-backed carpet, will suffice.

If the dog is restless, it may help to put on a collar and lead, and fasten the lead to an anchor-point fixed to the table. This leaves both hands free to deal with him – but many dogs resent being tied up. Whatever table is used, the dog must feel secure.

I like to have the tools I intend to use ready at hand, but I do not leave them where the dog can knock them off the table. Not all of the grooming tools will be used at any one session of trimming. To complete a dog for show can be a long and sometimes tedious job, depending on when he last had a show trim. A dog who is shown almost every week, and therefore kept in show trim, will need much less work and time spent on him than one who has not been trimmed for a month.

For hand trimming it is useful to have a chalk block within reach. Rubbing the forefinger and thumb on to the chalk helps to get a grip on the hair to be plucked out. It is also a great help to wear a thin rubber glove (thicker ones are not easy to work with), which makes plucking easier.

Initially, it is easier to have the dog sitting down, facing away from you. Work from the head backwards, with the No. 76 comb, and your thumb across the teeth of the comb, drawing the comb flat through the coat with slight pressure, and much of the loose hair will come out. A dog who has not been trimmed for a while may be in rather rough coat. To help remove a lot of the dead coat, I recommend combing with the wide-toothed comb with a wide rubber band threaded through it. It is surprising just how much hair this will remove.

Work can then be resumed with the No. 76 comb. Do this all over the dog first, then be prepared to work with the finger and thumb method. This is done by holding the skin taut with one hand, while with the other flicking the hair up in the opposite direction to which it grows, which shows up the longer hair. Longer hairs can then be plucked out, taking a few at a time. This may sound cruel to the inexperienced, but if done properly with the skin taut, it does not appear to hurt the dog or trouble him at all. This is where a rubber glove and/or chalk on the fingers really does help.

The above method should be used all over the top and back of the head, the top of ears, and then all over the body, before proceeding to the different parts of the dog, as follows.

HEAD
By holding the ears tightly under the throat, any long, straggly bits of hair on the head can be plucked out. If the dog is very untidy and hairy, this will take quite a while, but when it

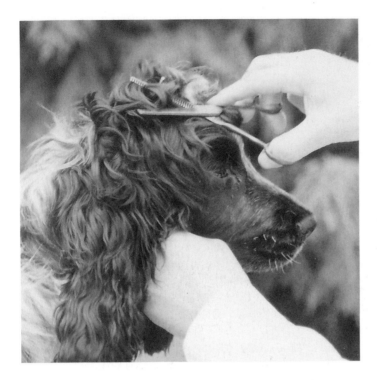

Thinning scissors can be used on the head of a pet if the dog is very untidy. However, for show, hand-trimming is the best method for long-term results.

is hand-trimmed and all the long, loose hair is removed, the head will have a very nice, long-lasting, smooth finish. If a 'quick-fix' method of using thinning scissors or a stripping knife is used, the immediate finish may look reasonably good, but it will grow back unevenly and will need repeating more often.

On the head, pay special attention to cleaning out all the long hair on the sides and back of the skull. If this is not removed, it gives the impression of the structure of the skull being heavier than it is.

EARS

First, comb the ears free of any tangles, both in the longer hair, and on the back edge where they lie closest to the head. If heavy tangles have formed, it may be necessary to break these apart with the tips of your scissors, taking great care not to cut the skin. Any cut skin will bleed, but ears seem to bleed more profusely than a cut on the body.

The hair on the top of the ears where they join the head should be plucked, as on the head. If too much hair is left on here, it gives the impression of the ears being set too high. Underneath, where the ears join the neck, you can use a comb to remove the majority of the loose hair, though most people use thinning scissors here to remove some of the hair and shorten the remainder, so as to help the ears to lie close to the head and neck. Only the tips of the scissors should be used, not the main body of the blades. The best way is to work in an upward direction, cut a little, then comb it out, and inspect the result before continuing, until the desired result is achieved.

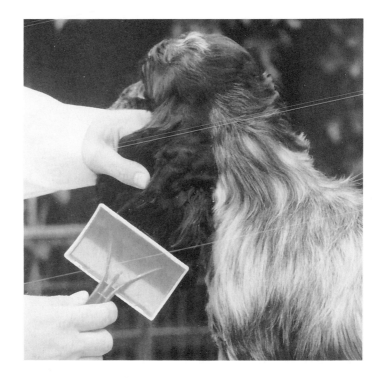

The ears must be free of tangles before starting to trim.

Use the finger and thumb method on the neck to achieve a nice, smooth outline.

NECK

This is perhaps the most difficult part to get right. The main aim of cleaning out all the long, straggly hair on the back of the neck, from where it joins the head to where it joins the shoulders, is to show up the length of neck and the line of the shoulders. Too much hair left on makes the neck look shorter. Combing with the No. 76, and using finger and thumb as described earlier, may take some time, but the results will be well worthwhile.

SHOULDERS

Continue from the join of the neck and on down through the upper forearm, so that the lay-back of the shoulder and the angulation of forearm can be clearly seen.

BODY

Using the same method, go over the body again, over the top of the back and down the sides about as far as in a line back from the elbows. Do not pluck out too much below this, which would remove some of the body feathering, but try to get the short body coat to blend in smoothly with the longer body feathering, and not leave a flounce standing out along the ribs.

HINDQUARTERS

Here you will find it necessary to use discretion and judgment about how much to take off and how much to leave on, as well as where to remove any excess. Nowadays, many of the blacks and dark blues grow somewhat thicker and heavier coats than they used to, with the result that people leave more hair around the stifle joint. The aim of trimming here is to show a good bend of stifle and good width of thigh, with the front of the lower

The hair can grow quite thickly on the hindquarters.

back leg cleaned out, and left visible. Hair left on in abundance down to the feet in a pyjama-like trim is unsightly and detracts from the overall picture of the dog.

On the back edge of the thigh, feathering is left on down to the hock joint, but the hair is shorter from that joint down the back of the lower back leg to the foot. The back of the lower back leg may be hand-trimmed first, then finished off neatly with thinning scissors.

After trimming, the dog should be moved away from the groomer, for him or her to watch and see that no long hair flaps around the hock joints, or gives the appearance of the hock joints turning in or out.

TAIL
It has always been accepted that to trim the tail completely by hand would be too painful for the dog. Any surplus hair on the top of the tail, and where it joins the back, can be removed by hand, but any excess length at the end of and underneath the tail may be removed with careful use of thinning scissors. Only a little at a time should be removed, until a neat appearance is achieved.

FRONT LEGS
The front and sides of the forelegs should be clothed in short hair, with any surplus removed by combing and the finger-and-thumb method. The back of the forelegs should be clothed in long feathering, but take care to see that no long hair flaps out at the sides of the legs, especially near the elbows. It is a good idea for the groomer to comb out the leg feathering, and then to get someone else to move the dog away and back, so that he/she can watch for any unsightly feathering which may make the dog's front look wrong. Hair left on in the wrong places can give an illusion of the dog turning its toes in (pinning), or being loose at the elbows.

THROAT
This is where the joining-up of trimming on the ears, back of neck, and upper forearm needs to be done first. If all these places have been done well, it makes the finishing-off easier to achieve. The throat is another place which has always been accepted as too tender for hand-plucking, and thinning scissors are normally used. By taking the scissors, and using the tips only, cutting in an upward direction along the undersides of the neck where it joins the throat, you will achieve a clean line when viewed from the side. The throat itself, and the hair on the lower part of the throat, should be thinned out in a V-shape from underneath the ears down to the breast-bone.

CHEST
If the dog is very heavily-coated, he may grow an abundance of feathering, with a lot of hair standing out in front. This should be gently tidied by hand if possible, and if not, a little thinning with scissors may be done. The aim should be for a judge to be able to see the dog's forehand construction, both when the dog is standing and when he is moving. If too much length of hair is left sticking out in front, it will also give an overall impression of the dog being longer than he actually is.

Excess hair underneath the tail should be removed using thinning scissors.

The throat is too tender for hand-plucking, so thinning scissors are used. Make sure you work in an upwards direction, using only the tips of the scissors.

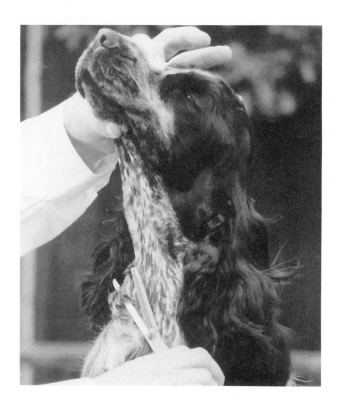

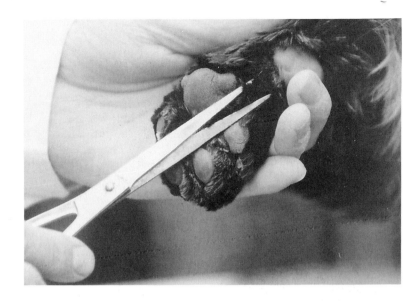

The surplus hair underneath the foot should be cut away.

FEET

Some dogs are sensitive about having their feet trimmed, so you should take care to see that nothing upsets the dog while this is being done. The easiest way is for the dog to sit while one foot is tidied up with scissors, by cutting all the surplus hair from around the sides of the foot, and the tufts over the top of the gaps between the toes (but not between the toes themselves). The foot should then be lifted and all the surplus hair underneath cut away, again taking care not to cut between the toes. When each foot has been done in turn, the dog should be made to stand in a show position, with his weight balanced equally over all four feet, and any odd bits of hair sticking out around or over the feet can be snipped away with the tips of the scissors. Always remember when trimming feet that the aim is to make them look as small, thick and well-padded as possible, and that, if too much hair is cut away, the wrong impression will be given.

FINISHING TOUCHES

Finally, the dog should be given a good smoothing-down with a brush or hound-glove (i.e. a mitten-shaped brush with wire bristles on one side and velvet on the other for polishing). Next, place the dog in a show pose, stand back and take a long look to see if the desired effect has been achieved.

Lastly, have the dog moved away, across, and back so that you can watch for any unsightly swing of the featherings and make final adjustments to your grooming. If all the hard work described above has been carried out – even if it has been done over two or three days in order not to overtire either groomer or dog – the end result should be very satisfying for the person who has done it.

Ready for the show ring: The Cocker Spaniel is now neatly trimmed, showing off her coat and conformation to full advantage.

There are many products which are sold as preparations to enhance the texture of the coat and maybe put an artificial shine on it. As mentioned earlier, a healthy, well-groomed Cocker will have a natural shine to his coat and such preparations should not really be necessary. However, here is a word of warning on the subject. There are Kennel Club regulations governing the use of any product which alters the natural texture or colour of the coat in any way. Coloured shampoos should not be used, as the regulations sanction the testing of hair samples for colouring, from dogs in pre-arranged breeds or classes. Details are not disclosed in advance of which breeds or classes will be checked. Anything which alters the texture must be fully removed before the dog enters the ring.

Chapter Four

THE BREED STANDARD

In this chapter I have set out two Breed Standards – English and American – for the Cocker Spaniel, together with a summary of the differences between them, and my own interpretation of the English Standard.

The Breed Standards should be regarded as descriptions of the perfect specimen of the breed, and are the yardsticks against which judging decisions are made.

THE ENGLISH KENNEL CLUB BREED STANDARD

GENERAL APPEARANCE
Merry, sturdy, sporting; well balanced; compact; measuring approximately same from withers to ground as from withers to root of tail.

CHARACTERISTICS
Merry nature with ever-wagging tail shows a typical bustling movement, particularly when following scent; fearless of heavy cover.

TEMPERAMENT
Gentle and affectionate, yet full of life and exuberance.

HEAD AND SKULL
Square muzzle, with distinct stop set midway between tip of nose and occiput. Skull well developed, cleanly chiselled, neither too fine nor too coarse. Cheek bones not prominent. Nose sufficiently wide for acute scenting power.

EYES
Full, but not prominent. Dark brown or brown, never light, but in the case of liver, liver roan and liver and white, dark hazel to harmonise with coat; with expression of intelligence and gentleness, but wide awake, bright and merry; rims tight.

EARS
Lobular, set low on a level with eyes. Fine leathers extending to nose tip. Well clothed with long straight silky hair.

MOUTH
Jaws strong with a perfect, regular and complete scissor bite, i.e. upper teeth closely overlapping lower teeth and set square to the jaws.

NECK
Moderate in length, muscular. Set neatly into fine sloping shoulders. Clean throat.

FOREQUARTERS
Shoulders sloping and fine. Legs well boned, straight, sufficiently short for concentrated power. Not too short to interfere with tremendous exertions expected from this grand, sporting dog.

BODY
Strong, compact. Chest well developed and brisket deep; neither too wide nor too narrow in front. Ribs well sprung. Loin short, wide with firm, level topline gently sloping downwards from end of loin to set on of tail.

HINDQUARTERS
Wide, well rounded, very muscular. Legs well boned, good bend of stifle, short below hock allowing for plenty of drive.

FEET
Firm, thickly padded, cat-like.

TAIL
Set on slightly lower than line of back. Must be merry in action and carried level, never cocked up. Customarily docked but never too short to hide, nor too long to interfere with the incessant merry action when working.

GAIT/MOVEMENT
True through action with great drive covering ground well.

COAT
Flat, silky in texture, never wiry or wavy, not too profuse and never curly. Well feathered forelegs, body and hindlegs above hocks.

COLOUR
Various. In self colours, no white allowed except on chest.

SIZE
Height approximately: Dogs, 39-4lcms (15.5-16ins)
Bitches, 38-39cms (15-15.5ins)
Weight, approx. 28-32lbs.

POINTS OF ANATOMY.

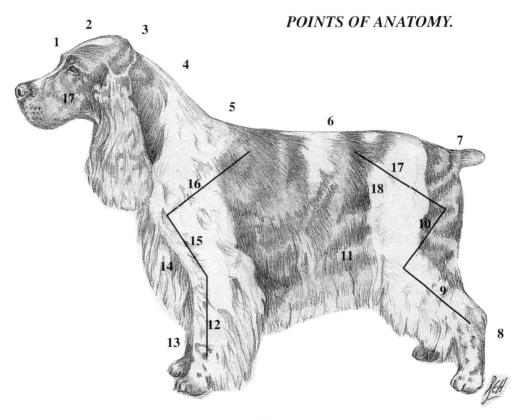

KEY

1. Stop
2. Skull
3. Occiput
4. Neck
5. Withers
6. Back and loin
7. Set-on of tail
8. Hock
9. Second Thigh
10. Upper Thigh
11. Abdomen
12. Forearm
13. Front pastern
14. Forechest
15. Upper arm
16. Shoulder
17. Haunch bone
18. Hip

FAULTS

Any departure from the foregoing points should be considered a fault, and the seriousness with which the fault should be regarded should be in exact proportion to its degree.

NOTE

Male animals should have two apparently normal testicles fully descended into the scrotum.

(Reproduced by kind permission of the English Kennel Club)

INTERPRETATION

When the Breed Standard was amended and re-published by the Kennel Club in 1986, it was intended to be a guideline for judges, and produced in the expectation that people reading it would already know something about the breed. It was shortened somewhat from the earlier Standard in order to fit in with headings to be used universally, but the changes were not intended to alter the breed in any way.

When a Breed Standard is consulted, everyone reading it has their own interpretation of what it is trying to portray, hence the difference of opinion between judges of dogs in competition. In order to expand on the Standard for less experienced owners, the following is my interpretation of the Standard, always bearing in mind the original purpose of the breed. This is based on experience gained from over 40 years in the breed. I shall always be grateful to the 'elder statesmen' who gave me the benefit of their knowledge and advice as I progressed throughout the years.

GENERAL APPEARANCE

"*Merry, sturdy, sporting; well balanced; compact, measuring approximately the same from withers to ground as from withers to root of tail.*"

This draws up a picture of a happy, robust, active dog, without any exaggerations, and with a square appearance from the neck back.

Int. Ch. Ouaine Chieftain showing a Cocker's sweet expression, which is a hallmark of the breed.

CHARACTERISTICS

"Merry nature with ever-wagging tail shows a typical bustling movement particularly when following scent, fearless of heavy cover."

To me this indicates a very active, busy dog, showing his enjoyment of the job in hand by wagging his tail as he hunts through hedgeways, woods and undergrowth. Not all Cockers are able to hunt in such conditions, as many live in urban areas nowadays, but the same hunting instincts and enjoyment can be encouraged merely by the owner hiding a favourite ball or toy, within reachable height for the Cocker's nose to scent it, and setting the dog the task of finding it.

TEMPERAMENT

"Gentle and affectionate, yet full life and exuberance."

I think this is an ideal description of a typical Cocker. It means that the dog can be gentle, show affection, and yet be happy and prepared for anything life offers.

HEAD AND SKULL

"Square muzzle, with distinct stop set mid-way between tip of nose and occiput. Skull well developed, cleanly chiselled, neither too fine nor too coarse. Cheek bones not prominent. Nose sufficiently wide for acute scenting power."

From this, I draw a mental picture of a dog with a well balanced head, with tip of nostrils and occiput equal in distance from the 'stop' or rise between the eyes. There should be good wide nostrils to allow the dog to use his scenting ability to the full. This usually goes with good width of nasal bone. Without this width of nasal bone, the muzzle itself will be too narrow. The skull should not be too wide – the width is normally accepted as being about the same width as that of the muzzle – and the cheek bones should be flat, not rounded or coarse.

THE HEAD

Typical head with good eye and expression, also showing good foreface and nostrils.

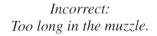

Incorrect:
Too long in the muzzle.

Incorrect:
Too short in the muzzle.

Correct: Well-balanced
muzzle and skull.

Incorrect:
The skull is too narrow.

Incorrect:
The skull is too wide.

Incorrect: The skull is too
rounded and heavy.

The word 'chiselled' in the *Kennel Club Glossary of Canine Terms* says: "Clean cut, showing bone structure of the foreface." I feel that in the reference to chiselling in the Cocker Standard, it not only indicates that the bone structure of the foreface should be clean cut, but also refers to the 'lift' over the eyebrows, which helps to create a balanced head and enhances the expression. A Cocker with a head lacking in chiselling, stop, and lift over the eyebrows has a very plain, untypical head.

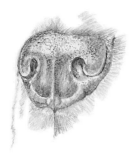

Correct:
Good width of nostrils.

Incorrect:
The cheekbones are too
prominent.

Incorrect:
The cheeks are too lean.

EYES

"Full but not prominent. Dark brown or brown but in the case of liver, liver roan or liver and white, dark hazel to harmonise with coat; with expression of intelligence and gentleness but wide awake, bright and merry; rims tight."

This is very descriptive, and indicates an eye which is neither deep-set nor protruding. The colour should be brown or dark brown, but in dogs of the liver colouring this is genetically impossible, so dark hazel is desirable. A liver dog with a 'gooseberry' coloured eye is not desirable. The term 'gooseberry eye' was common forty years ago when liver or liver roans were around, but there followed a period when these colours were rare, and the reference fell out of use. Now that the colour has had a resurgence of

THE EYES

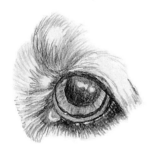

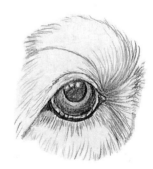

Correct:
Good eye and expression.

Incorrect:
The eye is too full and round.

Incorrect:
The eye is too small.

LEFT: The eye has an unpigmented third eyelid, which is regarded as a fault in some countries.

RIGHT: Undesirable: The loose lower lid shows the haw.

interest and is being seen quite often in the show ring, the 'gooseberry eye' should not be encouraged. The latter portion of the Standard speaks for itself.

I would add here that no reference is made in the Standard to the membrane commonly called 'the third eyelid'. That is the membrane at the bottom of the eye, but well inside the lower eyelid. If this is dark coloured, it does enhance the expression of the dog. In some particolours, this may be light coloured in one or both eyes, but if the expression is good, and the colour of the eye is correct, with no haw showing, this is acceptable.

EARS

"*Lobular, set low on a level with the eyes. Fine leathers, extending to nose tip. Well clothed with straight silky hair.*"

This means that the ears are narrower at the point at which they join the head than at the lower part of the ears. They hang low, but the point where they join the head should be level with the eyes. The fleshy part of the ears (the leathers) should not be thick and heavy, but fairly thin, and when stretched forward, the end of the leather (not the feathering on them) should reach to the tip of the muzzle.

THE EARS

Correct: The ears are well-placed, on a level with the eyes.

Incorrect: The ears are set too high.

Incorrect: The ears are set too low.

THE MOUTH

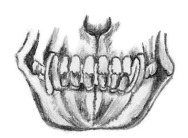

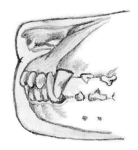

LEFT: Correct: Scissor bite, front view.

RIGHT: Correct: Scissor bite, side view.

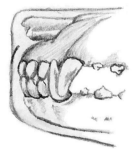

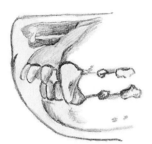

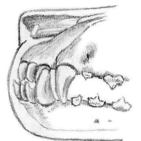

Incorrect: Level bite.

Incorrect: Overshot.

Incorrect: Undershot.

MOUTH

"Jaws strong, with a perfect, regular and complete scissor bite, i.e. upper teeth closely overlapping lower teeth and set square to the jaws."

The correct 'bite', as it is often called, is achieved by the upper jaw being slightly longer than the lower jaw, allowing the upper teeth to be slightly in front of the lower teeth. The teeth should not protrude or project forward at an angle, and they should be in line, not uneven. The upper teeth should close over the lower teeth like a pair of scissors, where one blade fits closely to the other.

NECK

"Moderate in length, muscular. Set neatly into fine sloping shoulders. Clean throat."

The neck in a Cocker should be well muscled – his original purpose in life was as a gundog to carry game. Without being well muscled he would never be able to carry a hare or large pheasant. The length should be in proportion to the rest of the dog, never too short and thick set, nor too long to create an impression of lack of balance throughout.

The throat should not have too much loose skin, but in my experience a dog with a good width and depth of muzzle will always have a little more 'throat' than a dog with a narrow muzzle.

FOREQUARTERS

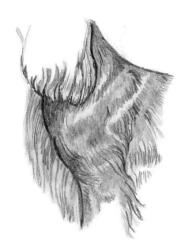

LEFT: Correct: Good
angulation of shoulder.

RIGHT; Incorrect: Too
upright in shoulder.

Correct: Good front with
correct width. This dog would
move correctly in front.

Incorrect: This front is
too wide.

Incorrect: This front is
too narrow.

FOREQUARTERS

"Shoulders sloping and fine. Legs well boned, straight, sufficiently short for concentrated power. Not too short to interfere with tremendous exertions expected from this grand, sporting dog."

The shoulders should be constructed with a good lay-back of the shoulder blade, and an equally good angulation of the upper forearm which places the front legs well back under the body. Not only should the shoulder blades be sloping well back, they should also be sloping inwards from where they join the upper forearm to the top of the shoulders, where there should be only one or a one-and-a-half finger-width between them.

Legs should be straight with firm round bone, which goes right down to the feet. Viewed from the side, the angulation should be obvious and, viewed from the front, the elbows should be well tucked in and not loose, which would show up when moving. The reference to "not too short" again comes back to the question of 'balance', where height and length of the dog are expected to be almost equal.

BODY

"Strong, compact. Chest well developed and brisket deep, neither too wide nor too narrow in front. Ribs well sprung. Loin short, wide, with firm level topline gently sloping downwards from end of loin to set-on of tail."

This indicates a strong dog, with a short, compact body structure. The need for a well developed chest and deep brisket was to provide plenty of heart and lung room for a working dog, in his original role. Nowadays many Cockers have insufficient width between the front legs, where there should be about a hand's width between the top of the front legs under the chest. This is usually coupled with little or no development of the sternum (or breastbone, often called the forechest) which is so desirable. Lack of development of sternum is often coupled with upright shoulder (lacking angulation or lay-back) and short upper forearms. Both of these are undesirable, and should be duly criticised. Fronts which are too wide are very obvious, particularly when the dog is moving towards you.

The ribs are well rounded and this can be seen clearly when you look down over the dog, and they go well back. The short, strong loin gives strength to the back, which in turn keeps the topline level, not only when the dog is standing, but when it moves too. There should be a good hand's width when the loin is spanned across the top; a narrow 'waistline' is not desirable. When the fingers are placed on the dog's side at the rear of the last rib, there should be only about three fingers' width to cover the length of loin – more length means the dog is too long in the couplings between ribs and hindquarters. Behind the loin, towards the set-on of tail, there should be a slight slope.

HINDQUARTERS

"Wide, well rounded, very muscular. Legs well boned, good bend of stifle, short below the hock allowing for plenty of drive."

The wide, well rounded rump of a Cocker, when he is moving away from you, should be sufficiently wide to obscure your view of any other part of his body.

He should be in hard, well-muscled condition, and his legs below the hock joint should be comparatively short, and at a right angle to the ground (not inclining underneath the dog, which is described as 'sickle hocks'). The lower back legs are commonly referred to as the hocks, but this is incorrect, as the hock is the joint between the second thigh bone and the lower back leg.

The angulation of the pelvis bone and thigh bone should be equal to the angulation of the shoulder blade and upper forearm – again I refer to the 'balance' of the overall dog.

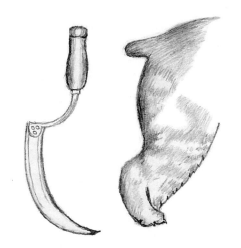

HINDQUARTERS

LEFT: Incorrect: Sickle hock.

BELOW: Incorrect: Sickle hocks seen when the dog is moving.

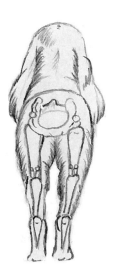

Correct hind conformation when the dog is standing.

Incorrect: Too narrow in hindquarters.

Incorrect: Too wide in hindquarters.

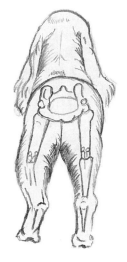  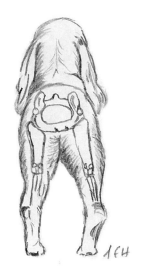

Correct width when the dog is moving.

Incorrect: Cow-hocked.

Incorrect: Hocks turning out.

Strong bone throughout will provide the ability to move with strength and drive.

The "good bend of stifle" referred to in the Standard comes from correct angulation. There should be good width of thigh, when viewed from the side. This is achieved when the angulation is correct and the muscle in the first and second thighs is well developed.

FEET
"Firm, thickly padded, cat-like."

A Cocker needs his feet to be thickly padded and to be closely knit together and well arched in order to work under rough conditions. Feet that have thin pads or spread, open toes would not allow him to work properly.

FEET

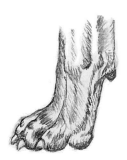

LEFT: Correct: A nicely shaped foot and a strong pastern.

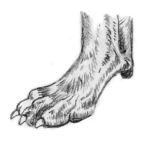

LEFT: Incorrect: This foot is too thin, and the pastern is weak.

RIGHT: Incorrect: The toes are too open – splay foot.

TAIL

"Set on slightly lower than line of back. Must be merry in action and carried level, never cocked up. Customarily docked but never too short to hide, nor too long to interfere with the incessant merry action when working."

The tail-set is very important, and it should be set slightly lower than the back, but carried on the same plane. It is most unsightly and detracts from the overall appearance and balance if the tail is carried up above the level of the back.

Normally, docking to about two-fifths of its original length will leave sufficient tail for the dog to use it and show his pleasure at what he is doing.

TAIL

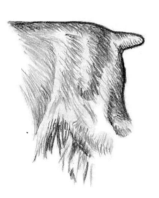

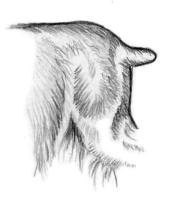

LEFT: Correct: Well set tail.

RIGHT: Incorrect: The tail is low-set.

LEFT: Incorrect: The tail is carried too low.

RIGHT: Incorrect: The tail-set and tail carriage are both too high.

MOVEMENT

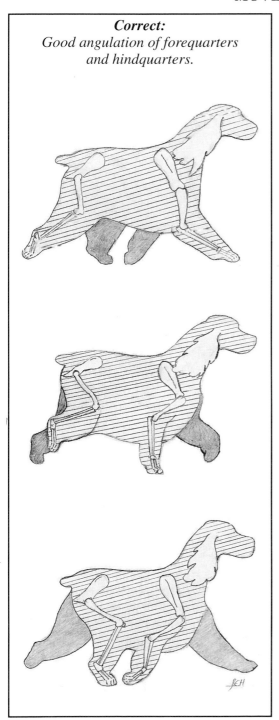

Correct:
*Good angulation of forequarters
and hindquarters.*

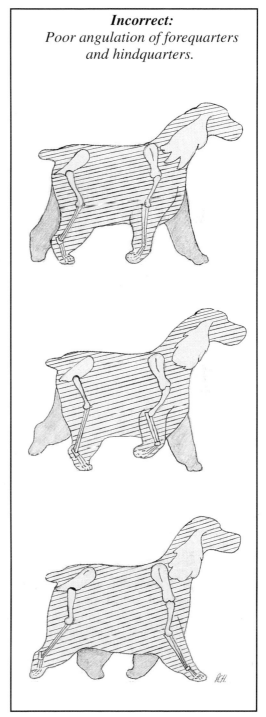

Incorrect:
*Poor angulation of forequarters
and hindquarters.*

ABOVE: Correct movement viewed from the side.

BELOW: Incorrect: Over-reaching. Note how one foot passes the other.

GAIT AND MOVEMENT
"True through action with great drive covering ground well ."

   This paragraphs depicts a dog who can move freely and cover a lot of ground with each stride. If he is properly constructed, when viewed from the side he will be able to reach well forward with front legs, and with good extension of the hind legs simultaneously. When the backward swing of the front leg is made, the rear leg comes forward, and the back foot should be placed just behind the front foot. If there is lack of angulation of the upper forearm, front reach will be restricted. Should this be coupled with greater angulation of the hindquarters, then when the back leg progresses forward, there will be insufficient space for it to go into, which will result in over-reaching. Dogs with correctly-set hocks and lower back legs, and good angulation, will propel themselves forward with the power coming from the hindquarters – otherwise known as 'drive'.

   Viewed from the front, the front legs should be parallel. The elbows should not be loose. Viewed from the rear, parallel movement is also required. The hock joints should not turn in or out.

LEFT: Incorrect: Front action is plaiting (or weaving).

RIGHT: Incorrect: Front action is too wide.

LEFT: Incorrect: The front is out at elbows.

RIGHT: Incorrect: The front action shows pinning.

Incorrect: Loose elbows seen when the dog is moving.

Correct:
The correct set of hindquarters give true, parallel movement.

Incorrect:
The hindquarters are too narrow, giving hind action which is too close.

Incorrect:
A cow-hocked dog, seen when moving.

Incorrect:
Hocks turning out, seen when the dog is moving.

Incorrect: The hind movement is too close and the hocks are brushing together.

Incorrect: This shows movement which is crabbing or crossing.

COAT

"Flat, silky in texture, never wiry or wavy, not too profuse and never curly. Well feathered forelegs, body and hindlegs above the hocks."

The texture of a Cocker's coat is important, and should be fine and silky, with a dense undercoat which is weather-resisting (and water-resisting for working or just enjoying being in water) and, as the Standard says, it should never be wiry, wavy or curly. The coat should lie flat to the body, and have nice fringes (feathering) down the back of the front legs, on the chest, under the ribs and stomach, around the stifle, and behind the back legs as far as the hock joint.

COLOUR

"Various. In self colours, no white allowed except on chest."

The word 'various' has given rise in recent years to all sorts of words being used to describe a dog's colour when Kennel Club registrations have been made. However, the generally accepted traditional colours are:

Black or liver, with or without tan markings.

Red or golden.

Blue roan, liver roan, black and white or liver and white, all with or without tan markings.

Orange roan, lemon roan, and orange and white, or lemon and white.

Many people nowadays refer to the liver colouring as 'chocolate', but I prefer the traditional description. When tan markings are present, they are usually seen inside the ear flaps, as thumbprint-size spots over each eye, on the muzzle, under the tail, and halfway up the forelegs and back legs below the hock. Sometimes they occur on the chest too, but these may be obscured by the feathering.

SIZE

"Height approx: *Dogs 39-4lcms (l5.5-l6 ins)*
                      Bitches 38-39cms (l5-l5.5ins)
                      Weight approx. 28-32lbs."

The height and weight suggested is not intended as a hard-and-fast rule, hence the word 'approximately'. Measures and weights are not used for Cockers in the show ring. A well boned dog, with plenty of substance and in good muscular condition, of 15.5-16ins will fit the standard weight of 28-32lbs, and a bitch in the same condition will comply at the lower end of the scale at around 28-30lbs. Many Cockers in the show ring in recent years have become smaller, and some have been fine in bone and would not come anywhere near the Standard in size or weight. Cockers of the correct size and weight tended to look larger than the others, and were often wrongly penalised for it. Fortunately, in the last couple of years the trend has been upwards – so maybe breeders are doing the right thing and trying to breed Cockers which fit the Standard in this respect, which means we shall soon have a ring full of correctly-sized, well boned, sturdy cockers.

FAULTS

"Any departure from the foregoing should be considered a fault and the seriousness with which the fault should be regarded should be in exact proportion to its degree."
NOTE: Male animals should have two apparently normal testicles fully descended into the scrotum."

According to the wording of the Standard, this is saying that anything which is not in accordance with the Standard is not correct – but that judges should not go overboard and condemn a dog entirely for any particular fault. They should look at the dog as a whole and then draw their conclusions.

However, there are a few faults which most judges would penalize heavily:
1) Undershot mouth or faulty dentition.
2) Monorchidism or cryptorchidism, where one or both testicles are missing.
3) Aggression or nervousness.

Another fault which many people dislike is a too-high tail carriage – this is very evident when the dog is moving and watched from the side view.

THE AMERICAN STANDARD
THE OFFICIAL STANDARD AS APPROVED BY THE AMERICAN KENNEL CLUB, OCTOBER 1988

GENERAL APPEARANCE
The English Cocker Spaniel is an active, merry sporting dog, standing well up at the withers and compactly built. He is alive with energy, his gait is powerful and frictionless, capable both of covering ground effortlessly and penetrating dense cover to flush and

retrieve game. His enthusiasm in the field and the incessant action of his tail while at work indicate how much he enjoys the hunting for which he was bred. His head is especially characteristic. He is, above all, a dog of balance, both standing and moving, without exaggeration in any part, the whole worth more than the sum of its parts.

SIZE, PROPORTION, SUBSTANCE
SIZE
Height at withers, males 16-17ins; females 15-16ins. Deviations to be penalised. The most desirable weights: males, 28-34 pounds; females, 26-32 pounds. Proper conformation and substance should be considered more important than weight alone.

PROPORTION
Compactly built and short-coupled, with height at withers slightly greater than the distance from withers to set-on of tail.

SUBSTANCE
The English Cocker is a solidly built dog with as much bone and substance as is possible without being cloddy or coarse.

HEAD
GENERAL APPEARANCE
Strong, yet free from coarseness, softly contoured, without sharp angles. Taken as a whole, the parts combine to produce the expression distinctive of the breed.

EXPRESSION
Soft, melting, yet dignified, alert, and intelligent.

EYES
The eyes are essential to the desired expression. They are medium in size, full and slightly oval; set wide apart; lids tight. Haws are inconspicuous; may be pigmented or unpigmented. Eye color dark brown, except in livers and liver parti-colors where hazel is permitted, but the darker the hazel the better.

EARS
Set low, lying close to the head; leather fine, extending to the nose, well covered with long, silky, straight or slightly wavy hair.

SKULL
Arched and slightened flattened when seen both from the side and from the front. Viewed in profile, the brow appears not appreciably higher than the back-skull. Viewed from above, the sides of the skull are in planes roughly parallel to those of the muzzle. Stop definite, but moderate, and slightly grooved.

MUZZLE

Equal in length to skull, well cushioned; only as much narrower than the skull as is consistent with a full eye placement; cleanly chiselled under the eyes. Jaws strong, capable of carrying game. Nostrils wide for proper development of scenting ability; colour black, except in livers and parti-colors of that shade where they will be brown; reds and parti-colors of that shade may be brown, but black is preferred. Lips square, but not pendulous or showing prominent flews.

BITE

Scissors. A level bite is not preferred. Overshot or undershot to be severely penalized.

NECK, TOPLINE AND BODY

NECK

Graceful and muscular, arched toward the head and blending cleanly, without throatiness, into sloping shoulders; moderate in length and in balance with the length and height of the dog.

TOPLINE

The line of the neck blends into the shoulder and backline in a smooth curve. The backline slopes very slightly toward a gently rounded croup, and is free from sagging or rumpiness.

BODY

Compact and well-knit, giving the impression of strength without heaviness. Chest deep; not so wide as to interfere with action of forelegs, nor so narrow as to allow the front to appear narrow or pinched. Forechest well developed, prosternum projecting moderately beyond shoulder points. Brisket reaches to the elbow and slopes gradually to a moderate tuck-up. Ribs well sprung and springing gradually to mid-body, tapering to back ribs which are of good depth and extend well back. Back short and strong. Loin short, broad and very slightly arched, but not enough to affect the topline appreciably. Croup gently rounded, without any tendency to fall away sharply.

TAIL

Docked. Set on to conform to croup. Ideally, the tail is carried horizontally and is in constant motion while the dog is in action. Under excitement, the dog may carry his tail somewhat higher, but not cocked up.

FOREQUARTERS

The English Cocker is moderately angulated. Shoulders are sloping, the blade flat and smoothly fitting. Shoulder blade and upper arm are approximately equal in length. Upper arm set well back, joining the shoulder with sufficient angulation to place the elbow beneath the highest point of the shoulder blade when the dog is standing naturally.

FORELEGS
Straight, with bone nearly uniform in size from elbow to heel; elbows set close to the body; pasterns nearly straight, with some flexibility.

FEET
Proportionate in size to the legs, firm, round and catlike; toes arched and tight; pads thick.

HINDQUARTERS
Angulation moderate and, most importantly, in balance with that of the forequarters. Hips relatively broad and well rounded. Upper thighs broad, thick and muscular, providing plenty of propelling power. Second thighs well muscled and approximately equal in length to the upper. Stifle strong and well bent. Hock to pad short. Feet as in front.

COAT
On head, short and fine; of medium length on body; flat or slightly wavy; silky in texture. The English Cocker is well-feathered, but not so profusely as to interfere with field work. Trimming is permitted to remove overabundant hair and to enhance the dog's true lines. It should be done so as to appear as natural as possible.

COLOR
Various. Parti-colors are either clearly marked, ticked, or roaned, the white appearing in combination with black, liver or shades of red. In parti-colors it is preferable that solid markings be broken on the body and more or less evenly distributed; absence of body markings is acceptable. Solid colors are black, liver or shades of red. White feet on a solid are undesirable; a little white on throat is acceptable, but in neither case do these white markings make the dog a parti-color. Tan markings, clearly defined and of rich shade, may appear in conjunction with blacks, livers and parti-color combinations of those colors. Black and tans and liver and tans are considered solid colours.

GAIT
The English Cocker is capable of hunting in dense cover and upland terrain. His gait is accordingly characterized more by drive and the appearance of power than by great speed. He covers ground effortlessly and with extension both in front and in rear, appropriate to his angulation. In the ring, he carries his head proudly and is able to keep much the same topline while in action as when standing for examination. Going and coming, he moves in a straight line without crabbing or rolling, and with width between both front and rear legs appropriate to his build and gait.

TEMPERAMENT
The English Cocker is merry and affectionate, of equable disposition, neither sluggish nor hyperactive, a willing worker and a faithful and engaging companion.

(Reproduced by kind permission of the American Kennel Club)

DIFFERENCES BETWEEN THE AMERICAN AND ENGLISH STANDARDS

When we compare the British Kennel Club Standard for the Breed and that accepted by the American Kennel Club, we can immediately see that the American Standard is rather more explicit, and worded more fully, than the British Standard. I think many British exhibitors of Cockers would do well to study the American Standard as far as forequarters, hindquarters, and gait are concerned – the intention is for the dog to be constructed and move just as we in Britain expect. Our own Standard is very brief in comparison. Both, however, stress that 'balance' is very important – rightly so in my opinion.

However, there are different requirements in the American Standard as far as topline is concerned. The wording: "The backline slopes very slightly toward a gently rounded croup...." differs from the British: "a firm level topline gently sloping downwards from end of loin to set on of tail".

This gives the impression of the American English Cocker Spaniel needing to have his topline sloping slightly all the way down the back from shoulders to croup, whereas the British Standard requires that from behind the shoulders to the end of loin, the back is firm and level – the slope being from the end of the loin to the set-on of tail.

There is a difference in the height and weight clauses too. In the American English Cocker, bitches are required to be from 15-16ins and dogs from 16-17ins. Deviations on size are said to be penalized. Compare this with the British Standard of approximately 15-15.5ins for bitches, and 15.5-16 ins for dogs.

This gives the American English Cocker two inches overall between the lower and upper limits, compared with the British range of approximately one inch. Weight for the American English Cocker is 26-32 lbs for bitches and 28-34 for dogs. Compared with the British Standard of overall 28-32lbs, this is fair enough. With an American upper weight limit of 34 lbs, this would balance out with the larger male of say 16.5ins. Clearly, if a dog of 16.5-17ins did not weigh 32-34lbs, he would be light in bone and substance, or very much underweight as far as 'body' goes.

Quite a number of breeders/exhibitors in the USA endeavour to maintain and promote the English-type English Cocker, particularly among the officers and members of the English Cocker Spaniel Club of America. There are many dogs of the American-type English Cocker too. A small number of the latter are also to be found in Argentina, Uruguay and Australia (to my personal knowledge, having judged them there). It has to be said that some of them are quite successful in the show ring, but mainly under visiting American all-rounder judges. They do not usually find favour under British judges.

For the benefit of readers who may not have seen this type – the so-called 'American-type English Cocker' – perhaps I should explain that, apart from being taller, they have a somewhat longer head, and the planes of the muzzle and skull are not parallel; the back-skull tends to fall away, and there is quite often a lack of distinct stop.

The back is sloping from shoulder to croup, and the hindquarters are usually over-angulated with a greater length from hip to hock than in the British type. This extra length means that when stacked in show pose, the front of the hind foot is well back behind the tail set.

When moving, they look quite impressive when viewed from the side, but are not sufficiently strong in the hindquarters when seen from the rear. The extra length from hip to hock seems to weaken the hindquarters, giving a too-close hind action, or showing looseness in the hocks.

Presentation of coat is somewhat different in the USA, being rather more 'shaped', with clipping of skull, and the top of and halfway down the ears, tightly trimmed on the body coat and in many instances a profusion of feathering especially on the chest. This does not really comply with the American Standard which says it should be done so as to appear as natural as possible. Having said that, American exhibitors (and the professional handlers in particular) do have the coats in beautiful condition and pay a great deal of attention to grooming and presentation.

For the enthusiast of the English-type English Cocker in the USA, any exaggerations are not acceptable, even though size may be a little different from Cockers on this side of the Atlantic.

In conclusion, I have to say that in Britain in recent years, many of the show Cockers have come down in size and substance (some of the bitches in particular) and are not in accordance with the Standard for size or weight. A dog of 16ins would appear too big compared with the others in the ring. Maybe we should endeavour to keep the British Cocker up to our own Standard requirements, and the American breeders should endeavour to keep the size of theirs down. Perhaps that way one day we shall achieve unity as far as Standards go. One can only hope!

Chapter Five

THE VERSATILE COCKER SPANIEL

GUNDOGS

Cockers make excellent shooting companions, whether for a day's shooting on what is known as 'Rough Shoot' (a day out in the fields, shooting a few pheasants, rabbits, hares, etc.), 'Driven Game' (a much more organised shooting party with several 'guns' and beaters driving the game forward, with or without dogs), or at a Field Trial, which is the top competitive form of gundog work at which a Cocker can compete.

While a dog's ability is something he inherits, the extent to which it is developed depends on the training he receives, and the ability of the trainer to bring out the best in the dog. For a Cocker to work at a Field Trial, he must show the following points:

a) That he is under control when off the lead.

b) That he is not aggressive towards any other dogs present.

c) That he will 'face cover', which means that he will hunt in rough undergrowth, brambles, etc. to find game and flush it out for the 'gun' to shoot.

d) That he is quick to respond to his handler's commands, which are sometimes by hand and often by whistle followed by hand signals.

e) That he has the ability to observe where the game falls when shot. When told by his handler to do so, he must retrieve it, tenderly, to hand.

TYPES OF COMPETITION

A Field Trial is the highest form of competition for a Cocker as a Gundog, but there are other tests such as Cold Game Tests, which are based on similar lines to Field Trials but using cold game, rather than hunting and finding live game and retrieving it when shot. At Cold Game Tests, as the name implies, cold game is used, and dogs have to find hidden or thrown game. This does encourage owners who lack the facilities to work their dogs on live game to try and maintain the working ability of their Cockers. The dogs enjoy it and so do the owners. These Cold Game Tests can be at various levels, from the beginners stage to that of the experienced dogs, thus encouraging owners to train their dogs to a high standard.

At Field Trials, a maximum of 18 dogs are allowed to run. Should there be more entries, a draw for places is held. There are two judges. Judge No.1 takes the odd numbers, and Judge No.2 the even numbers. An official 'gun' (someone to shoot the flushed game) is

The Cocker Spaniel is an excellent shooting companion. At four and a half months of age, this puppy is already retrieving from water.

allocated to each judge. At the completion of the required tests for the first dog, the judge then calls for the next dog, and so on till his list is completed.

After the first run, Judge No.1 then takes the even numbers and Judge No.2 takes the odd numbers, thus ensuring that both judges see all the dogs working. At the close of the second run, the judges compare their notes and make the awards, sometimes allowing a 'run-off', if two or more dogs are very close in their marks, to decide the final results.

When working, the dog should always be within hearing distance of his handler's signals and within gunshot range – there is no use in flushing a bird or hare too far away for the 'gun' to be able to shoot it. When working into a head-on wind, the scent of birds or ground game is fairly easy for a dog to pick up, and he will 'quarter' the ground (i.e. move in a fairly close zig-zag pattern), paying particular attention to areas where game is likely to seek protection such as bushes, nettles, brambles, etc., moving ahead of his handler, but always within gunshot range. When working with a following wind, a good dog will quarter the ground towards his handler from gunshot range. While the dog is doing all this, the judge will be watching to see how good the dog is at finding and flushing game, and retrieving.

For a Field Trial, the dog must stop immediately after he has flushed the game and wait for a command from his handler to retrieve it after it has been shot. He must not go to pick it up until sent to do so, but if his line of vision when seeing it fall is obscured, he may move forward a step or so to 'mark' (or make a mental note) of where it falls. If he 'runs in' (i.e. goes to pick up the game before the signal to do so is given) he will be disqualified.

On retrieving the game the dog brings it as directly as possible to the handler, who passes it, via the steward, to the judge, who will check for any damage to the game. This tells the judge whether the dog has a 'soft mouth', where no damage would occur, or is 'hard-mouthed' (most undesirable) and has crushed bones in the game. Retrieving a cock pheasant or a large hare means carrying a heavy weight for a small dog like a Cocker, and working Cockers usually have very strong neck muscles in order to carry the game holding their heads up.

FIELD TRIAL COCKERS

To earn the title of Field Trial Champion, a dog must have entered and won three Field Trials. Records for the Field Trials at which Cockers were entered during the 1993/1994 shooting season show that the following were among the winners of Open Stakes.

Mr P.W. Clulee's bitch, Wernffrwd Ammwyl (4).
Mr and Mrs P.E. and M. Jones' dog, Maesydderwen Kestrel.
Dr G.L.W. Cunningham's bitch, F.T.Ch. Laighpark Mist.
Lady P. Rhodes' bitch, F.T.Ch. Pixiebarn Gyp.
Mr J.D. Sowerby's bitch, Anahar Teuchat (2).
Mr D.C. Paterson's bitch, F.T.Ch. Anahar Tippit.
Mr A.C. McDonald's bitch, F.T.Ch. Kate of Swallowlaw.
Mr J. Holloway's bitch, F.T.Ch. Parkbreck Eagle.
Mr and Mrs G.R. and S.E. Watkins' bitch, Windmillwood Black Cherry (2).

LEFT: Hi-Jack Of Hilltop retrieving a rabbit, owned by Miss M.L. Doppelreiter in Austria.

BELOW: F.T.Ch. Nancarrow Carousel. Bred by Headley Millington, trained by Peter Jones, and in the ownership of Mr G. Tate in the USA.

ABOVE: F.T.Ch. Elan Greta, owned by Lt Cdr E.A.J. Collard.

RIGHT: Ch. Bowiskey Island Boy, owned by Mr & Mrs D. Bowkis.

Mr J.R. Bailey's bitch, F.T.Ch. Misty of Churchview.

Mr J. Shotton's dog, Chyknell Freckle.

Mrs C.E. Bellinger's bitch, Maesydderwen Kirsty of Ammerdown.

Lt Cdr E.A.J. Collard's bitch, F.T.Ch. Elan Garbo.

Mr P.S. Donovan's dog, F.T.Ch. Wenroc Swift.

Lt Cdr Collard's bitch, F.T.Ch. Elan Greta (2), one of which was the Spaniel Club Open Stake.

Mr M.R. Colclough's dog, Wernffrwd Cymro.

Mr R. Wales's dog, Parkbreck Jake.

Mr D.M. Douglas's bitch, F.T.Ch. Anahar Bawbee.

Mr G.W. Bowers' bitch, Lunnainneach Pepper.

Mr P. Jones' bitch F.T.Ch. Nancarrow Carousel (2), one of which was the Cocker Spaniel Championship.

At the time of writing, I have just heard that at the Cambridgeshire Field Trial Society's Open Stake on October 26th, 1994, the winner was Lt Cdr Collard's bitch, F.T.Ch. Elan Greta.

For those readers not familiar with Field Trial Cockers, it may be of interest to know that the Field Trial year runs from February 2nd in one year to February 1st in the next.

When Cockers first became a separate breed of Spaniel, most owners of the leading dogs not only worked them, but exhibited them too. Over the intervening years, there has grown a large gap between Field Trial-bred dogs and show-bred dogs, which neither side seems to have any incentive to overcome. The breeding of Field Trial dogs remains completely different from that of show Cockers, and I must admit, having seen Cockers working at a Field Trial, that they are very much faster in their work than show-bred dogs. They do not have the same build as show dogs either, and would not win in the show ring. Until the early 1970s, the Cocker Spaniel Club did put on classes at its Championship show for Field Trial Cockers but, sadly, there was little, if any, support and eventually the classes were dropped. It remains a pity that the two sides are so far apart as to be almost two different breeds.

SHOW COCKERS AS GUNDOGS

For Show Cockers, to win three Challenge Certificates brings the title of Show Champion, but to win the title of Champion (not as impressive-sounding, but much more prestigious), a dog has to show his working ability by demonstration, not in competition. This may be done at a Field Trial, but only if a dog has already won one or more CCs. Quite often, the two judges put the dog through his paces at lunchtime, after the first half of the Field Trial proper, when the dog must do all that is required of Field Trial dogs, except that he will not be disqualified if he 'runs in' and goes to collect the shot game a little before his handler's signal. Obviously, if he waits, so much the better.

To encourage owners to maintain the working ability of their show dogs, the Kennel Club in 1966 permitted a test called 'the Show Spaniels' Field Day' (inaugurated by the Midland English Springer Spaniel Club, but at which Spaniels of all breeds could compete). At this, dogs who had won a first prize at a Championship Show could run for a Qualifying Certificate, which would entitle them to their Champion title, if and when they won three CCs. The Field Day, as it is called, is held annually in October or November and it means that a dog whose working ability is of sufficiently high standard can win a Qualifying Certificate prior to winning his CCs, even if his owner does not have the facilities to train and run his dogs at Field Trials. This enables young dogs, not yet at CC level in the show ring, who show enthusiasm for working, to be trained at an earlier age than if the owners wait until CCs have been won. CC winners may also run at this event.

The first Show Spaniels Field Day was in the Midlands at the home of the late Lt Col Laurie and Mrs Kay Morris, who owned the Artistry Labradors and English Springers. The name Artistry was chosen as a prefix because Mrs Morris was a talented artist, painting under her maiden name of K.C. Brown. She would paint only Champions and Show Champions, and "dogs with funny little faces". Several Cocker owners are the proud possessors of one or more of her paintings (myself included, of my first Show Champion, Ouaine Parrandero, born in 1961). Sadly, Kay Morris died a few years ago.

There was an increased enthusiasm in the late 1960s and 1970s for qualifying show Cockers, including the now well-known stud dogs of the past such as Ch. Scolys Starduster and Int. Ch. Ouaine Chieftain, the record CC holder Ch. Bournehouse Starshine, and the late Arthur Mansfield's Ch. Lucklena Musical Director, and Ch. Lucklena Light Music. Mr Mansfield, who lived in a residential part of Derby, with an average-sized garden, achieved unique success by training and qualifying five of his Cockers to their Champion titles.

This achievement will be hard to beat, though Danny Bowkis from the Isle of Wight is keeping the flag flying, having qualified his two blue roan Champions, Ch. Bowiskey Boy Blue in 1991 and Ch. Bowiskey Island Boy in 1992. As Danny is young in comparison with Arthur Mansfield, let us hope that he will continue to train his dogs and win well in the show ring and, who knows, maybe compete with Arthur Mansfield's record. Joanna Walker also qualified her Ch. Okell Outward Bound in 1990 and Okell One for Luck in 1992, having won a Certificate of Merit at the Cocker Club Field Trial way back in 1963 with Blue Jay of Okell. The latest news is that at the Show Spaniels' Field Day in October 1994, Miss Walker obtained a Qualifying Certificate with her blue roan dog, Okell Oh Boy. I know from personal experience, having achieved a Qualifying Certificate with Int. Ch. Ouaine Chieftain and Ouaine Diana (who did not gain her Certificates to become a Champion but who was a really good worker), just how much time and patience it takes to train a dog to this standard. Anyone who does achieve such success is to be congratulated, not only for maintaining the working ability of their dogs, but for the effort made to prove that, given the opportunity, show Cockers can and will work well.

SHOW COCKERS ACHIEVING QUALIFYING CERTIFICATES
At Field Trials
Cocker Spaniel Club Field Trial, 24th November 1969: Mrs E.J. Caddy's blue roan dog, Ch. Ouaine Chieftain.

United Gundog Breeders' Association Field Trial, 6th November 1974: Mr G. Williams' blue roan bitch, Ch. Bournehouse Starshine.
Yorkshire Gundog Club Field Trial, 15th January 1977: Mr A. Mansfield's blue roan bitch, Ch. Silver Music of Lucklena.

At the Show Spaniels' Field Day
October 1966: Mr A. Mansfield's blue roan dog, Ch. Lucklena Musical Director.
October 1967: Mrs M. France's black bitch, Ch. Peeler's Cornbow Myth.
October 1968: Mrs D.M. Schofield's blue roan dog, Ch. Scolys Starduster;
                       and Mrs D. Owen's orange roan bitch, Ch. Saffron of
                       Settnor.
December 1969: Mrs E.J. Caddy's orange roan bitch, Ouaine Diana.
October 1973: Mr A. Mansfield's blue roan dog, Ch. Light Music of
                       Lucklena.
November 1974: Mrs K. Baldwin's black and white dog, Vailotest Savant.
October 1981: Mr A. Mansfield's blue roan dog, Ch. Lucklena Minstrel.
October 1990: Miss J. Walker's blue roan dog, Ch. Okell Outward Bound.
October 1991: Mr D. and Mrs C.A. Bowkis's blue roan dog, Ch. Bowiskey
                       Boy Blue; and Mesdames B. Rice-Stringer and J.P. Hook's
                       orange and white dog, Kennelbourne Spot On.
October 1992: Miss J. Walker's black and white bitch, Okell One For
                       Luck; Mr D. and Mrs C.A. Bowkis's blue roan dog, Ch.
                       Bowiskey Island Boy; and Mrs K. Cato's blue roan dog,
                       Okell Over To You.
October 1993: Mrs V. Cox's black dog, Luchriston Quick Step.
October 1994: Miss J. Walker's blue roan dog, Okell Oh Boy.

From the above results, it will be seen that since the start of the Show Spaniels' Field Day, the great majority of show Cocker owners who wish to run their dogs for a Qualifying Certificate do so there, rather than at a Field Trial. Having run dogs at both types of event, I can say that it was a most enjoyable experience trying a dog at a Field Trial, and although a lot of show Cocker owners feel that Field Trial people do not welcome show dogs, my husband and I were treated most courteously. We thoroughly enjoyed, before and after running our dog, seeing some of the best workers in the country competing.

After one of the European Spaniel Congresses held in England some years ago, we also saw some excellent working Springers showing their paces – again very enjoyable. However little space a Cocker owner may have, and even if a Cocker spends his life purely as a pet companion, it is possible to let him enjoy working, by retrieving a ball or stick in the garden or when out for a walk.

In order to help members to encourage their dogs, the London Cocker Spaniel Association holds training sessions, as well as Working Tests which give the dogs some form of competitive gundog work.

To see a Cocker working, whether in the field or garden, using his nose to follow scent and wagging his tail very fast on finding it, is a real pleasure. The dog enjoys it, and so should his owner.

THE COCKER AS A GUNDOG IN THE USA

Field Trials in the USA are run on much the same lines as those in the UK. There is no maximum number of dogs, but usually about 30 are accepted. At the last Field Trial, held by the English Cocker Spaniel Club of America, 28 dogs ran.

Field Trials for Cockers were held in the US until about the mid-1950s, after which they ceased for lack of interest. They restarted in April 1993, and ECSCA, as the national club, ran its first-ever Field Trial in September 1994. Trials were previously run by various breed clubs, but a Spaniel Trial can be run by any Spaniel Club.

There are only two types of Field Trials for Spaniels:
1) For Springers.
2) For Cockers, both American and English.

An American cocker ran in the first Field Trial in April 1993, but the rest were all English Cockers. A total of 28 ran, and only three were placed. Overall cover was apparently adequate, dogs ran reasonably well, and also did a water certification test.

To obtain a Field Trial Champion title, a dog must win two first-place awards in Open Stake, or one first place and ten points. Points are awarded thus: 2nd, three points; 3rd, two points; 4th, one point. A Water Test certificate is also necessary, but can be taken at any time.

A British Field Trial Champion, Omachie Tarf, a black dog born in March 1989, bred by Mr M. Forbes and exported to John R. and Sheila Courts became the first English Cocker to complete a Field Championship in America since the mid-1960s. He accomplished this by winning Open All Age Stakes at three of the four Cocker Field Trials offered under American Kennel Club Rules in 1993.

WORKING TESTS

WORKING DOG (WD)
WORKING DOG EXCELLENT (WDX)

These are Tests run by the National Club under their own Rules, and are not American Kennel Club Tests. These titles are not shown in show catalogues, except at the National Specialty, run by the National Club (ECSCA).

The Tests are performed with one dog and one judge. Either WD or WDX can be attempted. The result depends on performance under one judge. Natural instinct and ability is called for. WDX is for excellence of performance in all departments of the work, and can be achieved even when entering for WD.

The dog must work at least two, maybe three, birds at the discretion of the judge. He must flush and mark, but need not necessarily be steady to shot. He should mark well, retrieve with reasonable efficiency and within reasonable reach. For the 'Excellent' part of the award, he must retrieve to hand. A water retrieve is also called for. The dog may be gently restrained at the water's edge, but must go in eagerly, retrieve a bird from shot, and retrieve as on land.

These WD and WDX titles are held in great respect by Cocker enthusiasts, and, to mark the importance of the awards in keeping the Cocker instincts to the fore, ECSCA award beautifully-embroidered patches, which are worn with pride by the owners of the successful dogs.

HUNTER TITLES
American Kennel Club official tests are held for the following titles.
JH – Junior Hunter
SH – Senior Hunter
MH – Master Hunter

These are Spaniel Hunter programmes, and all Flushing Spaniels may enter. A specific class must be entered. No title is needed to enter, and entry can be at any level. No championship points are required to enter. The programmes are held to encourage people to get dogs into the profession and function of gundogs.

JH (JUNIOR HUNTER)
A dog must perform with two judges, and is judged against a standard from zero to ten. He must score more than five in every section, and an average of seven or more. A functional but good working dog is required. He must have bird-finding ability; must flush, but not necessarily be steady; must mark reasonably well and retrieve within reasonable reach (i.e. one step away); must show good working pattern, quartering adequately, covering the ground well, and perform a water test with a swim of about 20 yards.

SH (SENIOR HUNTER)
This requires a dog to be handled much less, doing all the above tests with very little assistance. He must also retrieve to hand, and must cover the field using his nose, using the wind, and going into cover. A blind retrieve to both dog and handler, of a dead bird, from about 15 yards must be performed. He must also do a water retrieve; the dog must be steady, and the distance is about 30 yards.

MH (MASTER HUNTER)
This requires a dog to be steady to wing and shot; cover adequately with barely any handling, using his nose and the wind, and going into cover. He must also do a blind retrieve and a water retrieve of up to 50 yards, and additionally a blind water retrieve which is sufficiently complex to sort the top dogs out. The blind water retrieve may have a bird on land after a swim, or in water, at the discretion of the judge.

All of these titles are highly regarded in the USA.

TRACKING
This activity is not carried out in Great Britain, but is very well supported in the

Can. OT Ch. Am. Can. Ch. Rose's Sherry Lenore Am. UDT, Can. UDTX., ECSCA WDX. This bitch finished her UDTX title at the age of twelve and a half years. Owned by Mrs. Sue Sellers Rose.

Scandinavian countries and in the United States by Cocker Spaniel owners and their dogs. The intention of Tracking tests is to make the dog use its scenting power – which is something all Cockers should have and enjoy using. These tests can be at various levels of competence. The American tests include the following exercises.

Exercises with the dogs hunting the scent of a human
TD: The track is about 500 yards in cover of fairly even type. At least two turns of any angle must be included, and the dog must locate a lost item at the end of the track. The handler usually walks behind the dog up to 20 feet in the rear, holding the dog on a 40-foot lead with a harness. The track will be from 30 minutes to two hours old, and is laid by a stranger to both handler and dog, at normal walking pace, with no scent path. The article to be found is laid on the ground at the end of the track, and must be indicated by the dog, or retrieved; either is acceptable.
TDX: This is more like a lost person search, and the terrain will vary (maybe tall grass, woods, ditches, fences, through gates, etc.), with four articles to be found – one at the beginning, two on the track, and one at the end. The track is about 1,000 yards long, with the scent three to five hours old, and will also have a cross-track with newer scent made by two different people crossing the track.

These tests are very good for letting the Cocker use his scenting power – even if he does not have the opportunity for field work as such.

There are several activities other than showing or gundog work in which Cockers can, and often do, take part. Some of these are very competitive, others are simply enjoyable for both dog and owner.

OBEDIENCE IN THE UK
Tests for competitive Obedience range from those for inexperienced or novice dogs, to those for very experienced dogs at Championship level. The requirements for Obedience Tests are:
Pre-beginners: This class may only be scheduled at Limited and Sanction and Open Obedience Shows.
Beginners: To compete in this class, owners, or handlers, or the dog must not have won a total of two or more first prizes in Beginners Class or one first prize in any other Obedience Class (Pre-Beginners Class excepted).
Novice: For dogs which have not won two first prizes in Obedience Classes (Pre-Beginners and Beginners Classes excepted).
Test A: For dogs which have not won three first prizes in Class A, B, and Open Class C in total.
Test B: For dogs which have not won three first prizes in Class B and Open Class C in total.
Test C: At Championship Shows, dogs must have won out of Novice, Class A, and Class B, and have won Open Class C on one occasion and been placed not lower than third on three occasions; all Open Class C places and wins under different judges.

Askonandy's Buccaneer CDX: Competing in two of the tests for the American CDX title. Owned by Dick and Jo Dixon.

The tests vary from Class to Class, and the higher the Class level, the higher the standard of work expected. There are numerous Obedience Training Clubs around the country which hold weekly training classes, at which dogs are trained and handlers taught how to get the best from their dogs. Much patience is needed, and frequent practice, but the togetherness it brings for dog and owner is very rewarding, quite apart from the joy of having an obedient dog.

OBEDIENCE IN THE USA
WORKING TESTS (CD and CDX)
CD (abbreviated from Companion Dog) and CDX (Companion Dog Excellent) are Obedience titles in the USA. Cocker Spaniel owners (English Cockers as they are called in America) are enthusiastic about working their dogs in several types of work, including CD and CDX. In order to achieve these titles, the dog must win three Qualifying Scores

under three different judges. A Qualifying Score is more than 50 per cent of points for each exercise, with a minimum total of 170 out of a possible 200. This means an average of 85 per cent accuracy.

For the CD Test the following must be carried out:

a) Dog must walk on lead with handler; make at least three stops (halt); change direction and make two changes of speed.

b) Do all the above off the lead.

c) Stand for examination by the judge, with the handler about six feet away.

d) Perform a recall of 30 feet from a Stay position.

e) Perform a long Sit for one minute and a long Down for three minutes with the handler at the opposite side of the ring. This is a joint exercise with other dogs.

For the CDX award, the following must be performed:

a) All the exercises detailed for CD Test.

b) Drop on Recall, with the judge directing the position of the drop.

c) Retrieve on the flat, 20 to 25 feet.

d) Retrieve over a high hurdle, one and a quarter times the height of the dog at the withers.

e) Perform a long jump which is twice the distance of the height of the high jump.

f) Long Sit (three minutes) and long Stay (five minutes) with handlers out of sight.

UTILITY DOG (UD) AND UTILITY DOG EXCELLENT (UDX)

These tests are very different from the CD and CDX Tests, and are much more complex. Some Cockers are worked in these tests, but more enter CD and CDX.

AGILITY

This is a comparatively recent form of competition, again at various levels, in which the dogs appear to have great fun, and need to be really fit and active, and the handlers also need stamina and speed. Obstacles of different types, such as jumps, ramps, tunnels, etc. have to be mastered by the dog, while the handler runs between the obstacles directing the dog to the next one. Speed is of the essence, and penalty points are awarded for errors such as a pole down on a fence. I have never tried my dogs with it, but Agility is always very exciting to watch.

I was privileged to be judging in Argentina in 1991 when the first Agility event in that country took place, at the Cocker Spaniel Club Championship Show. This took the form of a demonstration rather than a competition which included dogs of various breeds. To the enjoyment of Cocker owners at the show, a Cocker took part in the demonstration.

THERAPY DOGS

Known in the UK as PAT Dogs (Pets As Therapy), this is a really worthwhile task which involves the owner of a dog (which has to be of very good temperament) taking him/her to visit elderly, or sick, people who are no longer able to keep a canine companion of their own. Many residents in retirement homes remember with pleasure the times when they had dogs, and regret that it is no longer possible. For them the visits, usually once a week,

German Ch. Estee Lauder V. Osterreichring: A successful Agility competitor.

of a canine friend and owner, is a treat to which they look forward eagerly. In recent years, many owners of such homes, and the medical and nursing staff in geriatric hospitals, have come to appreciate just how much good such canine visits can do for the residents. Cockers, with their happy, outgoing nature, appealing expression, and wagging tails showing their pleasure too, are ideal for this purpose.

GOOD CITIZEN SCHEME

In order to promote responsible dog ownership, the Kennel Club introduced this scheme a couple of years ago. Dogs can be trained at home, or at Canine Society training classes, to the required level. Many clubs are taking part, and provide trainers and examiners for the tests, designed to prove that the dog is under control in different situations. Each dog proves how well it behaves individually, and not in competition with other dogs.

This scheme has had a very good reception from dog owners and canine clubs alike, and is doing a great deal to promote the rapport that is evident between an owner and a well-trained dog. It must also be seen as one way of combating the 'anti-dog brigade' which has been evident in many parts of the country in recent years.

In the USA, the American Kennel Club runs a similar scheme to the one outlined above. It is known as the CGC (Canine Good Citizen) scheme.

Chapter Six

THE SHOW RING

Successful showing requires a dog to be in good coat, fit, and in hard, well-muscled condition. He or she also needs to be properly trimmed, trained to walk purposefully and with drive on a lead, and, as important as anything else, to have a sympathetic and non-nervous handler.

The handler must have empathy with the dog. Temperament applies to the handler as well as to the dog. It is no use trying to browbeat a dog into doing what the handler wants. Both owner and dog must have the same objective and be in tune – all the time. The exhibitor must never show bad temper if the dog slips up, because encouragement is the name of the game. Enjoyment for both is the result of sympathetic handling.

First of all, ask yourself: "Why show? Why not be satisfied with love and companionship from my dog?" The answer to this question is that, in showing, both owner and dog benefit, the owner from the pride of ownership and the satisfaction of winning, and the dog from the love of going to shows – win or lose. I know that my dogs all look forward to it. Winning is not a certainty. There are many more losers than winners, especially in a numerically strong breed like Cockers. An exhibitor has, therefore, to be prepared to lose more often than he wins. There is no point in getting exasperated or blaming the judge. If you cannot take losing, then you are better off not showing. The reasonable exhibitor gets pleasure from showing his favourite dogs, and from the friendship of other exhibitors.

REQUIREMENTS FOR SHOWING
What is required? Obviously, you need a reasonably good dog whose construction is near to the Breed Standard. If you are a newcomer to showing, it is easy to read that Standard and to think that your dog is a world-beater. You will be very lucky if he is. You must be able to understand fully what the Standard is calling for in all its aspects, and not just on the particular points on which your dog scores well.

Then there is the comparison with the other dogs in your class. Sometimes they will be very good, and sometimes not so good. The easiest thing in the world is to stand outside the show ring and, with complete ignorance, find fault with the placings of the judge. The really hard job comes when you actually have to handle them yourself, and then assess their merits.

The novice owner can be forgiven for believing that his dog is the best in the world. It could easily be so, but not necessarily in a beauty competition. Before showing, it would be best to ask an experienced breeder for a general assessment. The easiest way is to go to a show, preferably a show confined to Cockers where there will be more of them to see, and to ask someone whose dogs appeal and are well placed. Obviously this should be done at an appropriate time (not when an exhibitor is just getting his dogs ready for the ring).

Having acquired your dog, it must be registered and transferred at the national Kennel Club before it can be shown, not until the age of six months. Personally, I think it unwise to show a puppy until it is reasonably well-developed, not nervous, and lead-trained. If it is to have a fair chance, it must also look its best. Show trimming is not easy and only practice makes it perfect, or as near perfect as possible. You cannot expect to get it right first time, and you will have to be able to recognise where to take off hair, or leave it on, to emphasise good points or cloak bad points. As an example, hair left on and shaped around the stifle can often disguise straightness. The hands of the judge should tell him how good or bad the dog is, but it is up to him to find out. First impressions count, and the first impression the judge has of your dog should be as good as possible.

Next comes training, both for yourself and for the dog. Nervousness on the part of the exhibitor transmits itself down the lead to the dog. If you are worried, your dog will be too. Show, or Ringcraft, training classes are held by many canine societies, often on a weekly basis, and it is advisable to practise there. These are good training sessions, not only for the dog, but for the handler to learn how to get the best from his dog. Ringcraft training classes should be distinguished from Obedience training classes, where emphasis is on competitive Obedience and at which a dog is taught to sit immediately the owner stops walking. This would not be suitable for the show ring.

IN THE RING

When a Cocker is shown, it is usually 'set up', or posed, to allow the judge to see the dog. Obviously you want him to see the good points of a well-balanced dog. Training classes should show you how to do this. The Kennel Club does not allow a lead to be taken off during a show. It should be draped over the shoulder of the dog. If it is left halfway up the neck, it gives the visual impression of a stuffy or over-short neck. Cockers are normally placed on a table for the judge to run his hands over the dog, and a puppy should be practised in allowing people to handle him (such practice is also given at training classes). After that, the judge will ask the handler to move the dog. This entails either going in a straight line across the ring and back, or moving in a triangle. The object of this exercise is for the judge to see that the front and back legs move in a straight line. From the side he will see whether the topline is level (as it should be) as the dog moves, and that both his front legs and back legs are moving with power. Short, choppy steps are not what is required. For a small dog, a Cocker should be able to cover a lot of ground with each stride. It is easy to feel that a judge should excuse any shortcomings he finds in your dog and penalise others for the same fault. No dog is perfect and you have to learn to accept decisions, good or bad. Be happy when you win, but do not get bad-tempered when you lose. If you cannot lose gracefully, it is better for everybody for you to stay away.

If you are a beginner, take advice on which of the many classes the dog should be entered in. At Championship shows, dogs placed in some of the classes earn the right to be shown at the Mecca of dog shows – Crufts. It is lovely to be there, but remember that a lot of other people would also like to be there, which means considerable opposition in those classes.

In many countries, dogs are lined up in numerical order and the numbers mostly relate to the alphabetical order of the names of the owner. Thus Mrs Atkins will be seen early on in the class and Mr Zebedee at the end. In Britain, you can stand anywhere in the line, in no particular order. If you are new, I would advise standing in the middle and watching carefully what the regulars do. You can talk to your neighbour while judging is going on, but you should not let your attention wander from your dog. If the judge happens to look across he must not see the dog looking his worst.

Abroad, exhibitors try to look as smart as their dogs and dress accordingly. Over here, in latter years, standards of dress have fallen. Remember, however, that if you do win Best of Breed at a Championship Show, you will be a contender in the Group. Would you want to look scruffy there? Being smart does not necessarily mean being dressed in the height of fashion, and long floaty skirts tend to obscure the judge's view of the dog when moving, and maybe distract the dog too. Clothes should be comfortable to move in, and of a colour to enhance your dog. For example, do not wear a black skirt or trousers when standing a black dog in front of them – it does not show up the dog, just obscures it. Light colours show up a black dog better. Plain colours show up a particoloured dog best. All these small points help towards showing a dog to its best advantage.

Much of this chapter has been devoted to things that the regular exhibitor takes for granted. However, I would like to say to all seasoned exhibitors: "You were new at the game once, so spare a sympathetic thought for comparative newcomers to the game and help them if you can. Without them, there would be no dog shows for you."

TYPES OF SHOW

There are several types of shows, all of which are run under Kennel Club Rules and Regulations. Starting at the lowest level and moving up to the highest, the various British shows are as follows.

EXEMPTION SHOWS

Usually run in aid of a charity or other worthy cause, these consist of four classes for pedigree dogs (which need not necessarily be Kennel Club registered), and a number of 'novelty' or fun classes. These are useful for new exhibitors to try out their handling, and to introduce the dog to showing. They are also used by regular exhibitors, mainly to give practice to new youngsters.

SANCTION SHOWS

This type of show was very popular some years ago, but not many are held now. They are restricted to dogs who have not been top winning (dogs up to Post-Graduate standard only may be shown) and are mostly for dogs of all breeds.

LIMITED SHOWS

These can be All Breed shows, or confined to one breed. They are limited, as the name implies, to members of the club or society running the show. Dogs who have won Challenge Certificates (or any award which counts towards the title of Champion under other ruling bodies, e.g. the Irish Kennel Club) are not eligible to be shown at this type of show.

OPEN SHOWS

These too can be All Breeds, one breed, or even one Group shows (e.g. all gundogs). All dogs, even Champions, may be shown.

Entries for all shows, other than Exemption shows, close in advance, and details of the venue where the show is to be held, date of closing of entries, etc. can usually be found in advertisements in the canine press. Judges for all the above shows, Exemption, Sanction, Limited and Open, are selected by the committee of the organising body, and do not have to be approved by the Kennel Club.

CHAMPIONSHIP SHOWS

Some are for All Breeds, some for one Group, and some for one breed. All dogs aged six months upwards are eligible to enter. Classes are usually provided for Minor Puppies (six-nine months), Puppies (six-twelve months), Juniors (six-eighteen months) and then classes are graded according to the amount of winning dogs have done. For Cockers, it is usual for classes to be divided, with dogs and bitches being shown separately.

At these shows, Challenge Certificates are offered for Best Dog, and Best Bitch, and three of these much-coveted awards, won under three different judges, enables a dog (after Kennel Club approval) to be called Show Champion.

Judges for Championship shows are selected by the committee of the organising body, but have to be approved by the Kennel Club on every occasion, and may not judge the same sex of that particular breed again within a period of nine months. The Kennel Club has decreed that, as from January 1996, the period shall be increased to 12 months.

The number of Championship shows per year for any breed is controlled by the Kennel Club, and based on calculations including the number of registrations in that breed and the number of dogs actually shown at Championship shows during the preceding three years. In 1994, there were 46 Championship shows for Cockers, but for 1996, which is the latest allocation made by the Kennel Club at the time of writing this book, Cockers will have only 38 Championship shows. This will make it even more difficult to achieve the title of Show Champion or Champion. By reducing the numbers of CCs on offer, the Kennel Club's intention is to maintain a very high standard of dogs winning the title of Sh. Ch. or Ch.

BECOMING A CHAMPION IN THE US

In the US the system differs somewhat as points are the basis used for achieving champion status. As in the UK, the sexes are divided. and at least three different judges are required to give the requisite number of points (fifteen) to make a Champion. The championship points are given for Winners Dog and Winners Bitch and the number of points given at a particular show will depend on such things as the number of dogs competing in your breed. The number of points varies in different parts of the country, but a list is printed in the catalogue for every show. The maximum number of points that it is possible to win at one show is five, and this would be considered to be a major. To become a champion, a dog must win at least two majors under different judges.

CRUFTS WINNERS
Crufts is regarded throughout the world as the summit of dog showing, and it is every exhibitor's dream to win the Best of Breed award (if not higher) at this show. A few of the dogs and bitches winning Best of Breed at Crufts in the last 25 years have gone on to higher wins.

No recent owner has matched the achievements of Mr H. S. Lloyd who won Best in Show All Breeds six times during the 1930s and 1950s – twice each with Lucky Star of Ware, Exquisite Model of Ware, and Tracey Witch of Ware (who very nearly made it a unique record of three times, but just missed out and ended up with twice Best in Show and once Best Bitch in Show).

Some notable Crufts wins have been:
1969: Sh. Ch. Lochranza Strollaway won the Gundog Group and Reserve Best in Show.
1970: Int. Ch. Ouaine Chieftain won the Gundog Group and Reserve Best in Show.
1978: Sh. Ch. Lochranza Man of Fashion won the Gundog Group.
1994: Sh. Ch. Lynwater Dawn Shimmer won the Gundog Group.

CRUFTS BOB WINNERS 1969-1995

1969 Sh. Ch. Lochranza Strollaway: Best of Breed, winner of the Gundog Group, and Reserve Best in Show. Owned By Miss J. Macmillan & Mrs. J. Gillespie.

Photo: Thomas Fall.

RIGHT: 1970 Ch. Ouaine Chieftain: Best of Breed, winner of the Gundog Group, and Reserve Best in Show. Owned by Joyce Caddy.

Photo Diane Pearce.

LEFT: 1971 Sh. Ch. Merryborne Simone: Best of Breed. Owned by Irene Martin.
Photo: Anne Roslin-Williams.

BELOW: 1973, 1975 and 1976 Ch. Bournehouse Starshine: Best of Breed. Owned by G.F. Williams.

ABOVE: 1974 Sh. Ch. Janeacre Night Skipper of Helenwood: Best of Breed. Owned by Mrs J. Marris-Bray.

LEFT: 1978 Sh. Ch. Lochranza Man Of Fashion: Best of Breed and winner of the Gundog Group. Owned By Miss J. Macmillan & Mrs J. Gillespie.

RIGHT: 1980 Sh. Ch. Bryansbrook High Society: Best of Breed. Bred by Mr and Mrs B. Fosbrook (later Am. & Can. Ch. when owned by Mr E. Phoa).

BELOW: 1982 Sh. Ch. Helenwood Capelle: Best of Breed. Owned by Mrs J. Marris-Bray.

ABOVE: 1981 Sh. Ch. Craigleith The Waltz Dream: Best of Breed. Owned by Mollie Robinson.

1983 Sh. Ch. Roanwood Ripple: Best of Breed. Owned by Mr & Mrs R. Clarke.

1984 Sh. Ch. Cilleine Echelon: Best of Breed. Owned By Mrs D. Barney.

Photo: Dave Freeman.

1985 Sh. Ch. Matterhorn Montana: Best of Breed. Owned by Mr H. Jones.

Photo: Gerwyn Gibbs.

*1986 Sh. Ch.
Haradwaithe
Sorceress: Best of
Breed. Owned by
Mr S. Clayforth
and Mr R. Peters.*

*Photo: Roger
Chambers.*

*LEFT: 1987
Sh. Ch.
Courtmaster
Abracadabra:
Best of Breed.
Owned by Mr
& Mrs D.
Telford.*

*1988 Judika
Blackamour: Best of
Breed. Owned by Mr &
Mrs K. Costello.
Photo: Alan V. Walker.*

RIGHT: 1989 Sh. Ch. Roanwood Flint: Best of Breed. Owned by Mrs S. Clarke.
Photo: John Hartley.

CENTRE: 1990 Ch. Bowiskey Boy Blue: Best of Breed. Owned by Mr & Mrs D. Bowkis.

BOTTOM RIGHT: 1991 Sh. Ch. Charbonnel Fair Cher: Best of Breed. Owned by Mrs S. Platt.
Photo: David Bull.

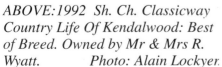

ABOVE: 1992 Sh. Ch. Classicway Country Life Of Kendalwood: Best of Breed. Owned by Mr & Mrs R. Wyatt.
Photo: Alain Lockyer.

1993 Sh. Ch. Lujesa Fiore Dorato: Best Of Breed. Owned by Misses S. & A. Kettle.

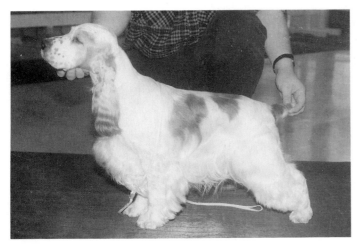

1994 Sh. Ch. Lynwater Dawn Shimmer: Best of Breed and winner of the Gundog Group. Owned by Mrs E. Maclean.

1995 Sh. Ch. Quettadene Mystique: Best of Breed. Top Cocker 1994. Owned by Mrs P. Lester. . Breed record holder for blacks with 38 CCs.

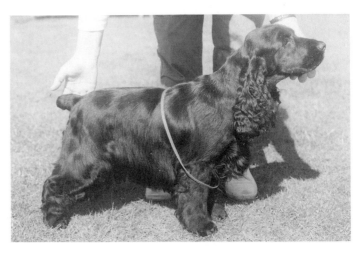

OTHER TOP WINNERS

Many other Crufts Best of Breed winners have gone on to attain their titles, if they had not already done so, and some became Cocker of the Year.

Apart from Crufts, times have changed in the last 25 years, or maybe the Cockers have, but nowadays Cockers do not seem to hit the high spots in the show ring as often as they did previously. Some who have gone further than gaining their Ch. or Sh. Ch. titles and have won Groups or Best in Show All Breeds during the last 25 years, have been:

Sh. Ch. Lochranza Strollaway (black dog): Winner at Crufts in 1969 but later exported to Argentina and thus lost to British shows.

Int. Ch. Ouaine Chieftain (blue roan dog): Res. BIS Crufts 1970, Best in Show All Breeds at Paignton and SKC (Scottish Kennel Club) Ch. Shows, winner of seven Groups and five Green Stars under IKC (Irish Kennel Club) rules.

Mr and Mrs J. Smith's Sh. Ch. Sorbrook Holly Berry (rcd bitch): Group winner at Belfast Ch. Show.

Mr and Mrs Webster's Sh. Ch. Asquanne's Genevieve (black bitch): won the Group and Res. Best in Show at Paignton in 1993.

Ch. Bournehouse Starshine (blue roan bitch): several Groups and four BIS wins at All Breed Ch. Shows.

The late Margaret Stevens' Raneyl Late Summer of Leabank (blue roan bitch): Gundog Group at WELKS (West of England Ladies' Kennel Society).

Mrs D. Barney's Sh. Ch. Cilleine Echelon (blue roan dog): four Groups; three Res. BIS at Group Shows; and three Res. BIS at All Breed Ch. Shows.

Penny Lester's Sh. Ch. Quettadene Emblem (black dog): winner of five Gundog Groups including BIS, Gundog Breeds of Scotland, 1984 and Res. at SKC in the same year; Group and Res. BIS, Blackpool 1985. Top Gundog 1985. Sire of nine Sh. Chs. and several other CC winners.

May Snary's Sh. Ch. Platonstown Scooby Doo (black dog): BIS All Breeds, Belfast Ch. Show.

Mr and Mrs Ernie Darby's Sh. Ch. Classicway Cutty Sark (blue roan dog): BIS at Gundog Club of Wales Ch. Show: the same owners' Sh. Ch. Classicway Cressida, (blue roan bitch) was Res. Gundog Group at WELKS, and Midnight Blue Horizon won the Gundog Group at Bath, 1989.

Mr K. McFarlane's Sh. Ch. Maxway Music Maker (blue roan dog): BIS All Breeds, Three Counties Ch. Show, 1987.

Mrs Holmes' Sh. Ch. Kenan Rick O' Shea (black dog): won Gundog Group at Paignton in 1988.

Mr Moray Armstrong's Sh. Ch. Bitcon Troubador (blue roan dog): BIS National Gundog Ch. Show 1992.

Mr and Mrs Ron Clarke's Sh. Ch. Roanwood Flint (black dog): winner of Gundog Group at Paignton 1991.

Penny Lester's Sh. Ch. Quettadene Desdemona (black bitch): winner of Gundog Group and Res. BIS at Driffield Ch. Show, 1993.

NOTABLE ACHIEVEMENTS
The following are a few exceptional achievements within the breed which spring to mind as I write:

Richmond Weir (Weirdene) has the unique distinction of having made up Show Champions in six different colours.

The late Arthur Mansfield qualified in the field and made all his six blue roans into full Champions.

The only red Cocker ever to win Best in Show at an All Breed Championship Show was the late Judy de Casembroot's Treetops Turtle Dove. Though this was well before the period covered by this book, it deserves a mention.

The record number of CCs won by a Cocker in Britain is 61, won by the home-bred bitch Ch. Bournehouse Starshine. The late Alf Collins held the record for the highest number of CCs won by a dog (59) with Ch. Colinwood Silver Lariot. This record still stands. As Lariot was not home-bred, the record number of CCs won by a home-bred dog (36) is held by Sh. Ch. Cilleine Echelon (who took over from my own Ch. Ouaine Chieftain (32), who in turn took over from the late Joyce Gold's lovely blue roan dog, Ch. Oxshott Marxedes (26). It is interesting to note that all of these top winners were blue roan, and all except Echelon were full Champions.

During her long show career, Ch. Bournehouse Starshine produced two Show Champions in one litter, Gordon Williams' Sh. Ch. Bournehouse Shine On and John Oulton's Sh. Ch. Bournehouse Silver Star. Not many bitches have produced two Champion children, and I am proud of the fact that my own black and white bitch Ouaine Panderosa produced not only Int. Ch. Ouaine Chieftain by Crackshill Tricolour of Ide, but also the black, white and tan dog, Sh. Ch. Ouaine Chipaway (six CCs, three Res. CCs) to Waylight of Weirdene.

Sh. Ch. Lochranza Quettadene Marksman: Best of Breed and winner of the Gundog Group, Crufts 1967. Owned by Miss J. Macmillan & Mrs J. Gillespie.

TOP LEFT: Sh. Ch.
Platonstown Scooby Doo: Best
in Show at Belfast Ch. Show
1984. Owned by Mrs M. Snary.

ABOVE: Sh. Ch. Quettadene
Emblem: Winner of five
Gundog Groups, including BIS
at Gundog Breeds of Scotland
Ch. Show, and two Reserve BIS
All-Breed wins at Ch. Shows.
Owned by Mrs P. Lester.
Photo: Anne Roslin-Williams.

ABOVE: Sh. Ch. Quettadene
Desdemona: Winner of
Gundog Group and Reserve
Best in Show, Driffield Ch.
Show 1993. Owned by Mrs P.
Lester.

RIGHT: Sh. Ch. Bitcon
Troubador: Best in Show,
National Gundog Ch. Show
1992. Owned by Mrs K.
Armstrong.

*Sh. Ch. Kavora
Merryborne Sweet
Martini: Record
holder for CCs (19)
won by a red or
golden Cocker.
Owned by Miss P.
Trotman.*

*Sh. Ch. Asquannes
Grainne: Former
record holder for
CCs (36) won by a
black Cocker.
Owned by Mr &
Mrs A. Webster.*

Referring to bitches with more than one title-holding progeny caused me to look a little closer at my records, and from these I found the following:

Irene Martin's red bitch, Lochranza Honeyglow, produced two.

The late Dorothy Hahn's black bitch, Sweet Rebecca of Misbourne, produced two.

Sheila Sadler's bitch, Misbourne Sweet Lizbie, was the mother of two blacks from one litter, Sh. Ch. Rosaday Super Trooper and Sh. Ch. Rosaday Leading Lady.

Matterhorn Masquerade, owned by Mr H. M. Jones, produced two black and white Sh. Chs.

The black bitch, Olanza Princess Gem, owned by Miss P. Becker, was the dam of littermates Sh. Ch. Olanza Poachers Moon and Sh. Ch. Olanza Promise Me.

The late Mrs Doxford's red bitch, Butter Candy of Broomleaf, was the dam of litter sister and brother, Sh. Ch. Broomleaf Bright Memory and Sh. Ch. Broomleaf Black Silk.

Sue Young's bitch Sh. Ch. Canyonn Christa was the dam of two.

Miss Wormell's Sh. Ch. Lynwater Tawny Owl produced two.

Jacky Marris-Bray owned the red bitch Sh. Ch. Helenwood Capelle, who was the dam of three Sh. Chs., two red bitches, Amerella and Oryelle, and the black dog Avalaf. She followed that with another CC winner in the red bitch Spot the Difference.

In particolours, Mr M. Armstrong's Hightrees Love Serenade produced two.

Lt Cdr and Mrs Blake's Sh. Ch. Cochise Circe was the dam of two, and the same owners' Cochise Caparica also produced Sh. Ch. Cochise Chirichua and Sh. Ch. Cochise Cshakira in the same litter.

Mr and Mrs Darby must be proud of the fact that not only did their blue roan bitch, Adargi Joyful Girl of Classicway, produce two from one litter, and another from a later litter, but her daughter Sh. Ch. Classicway Carrie Ann has also produced three Sh. Chs., one of which won Best of Breed at Crufts in 1992.

The record number of CCs won by a red is held by Pam Trotman's bitch, Sh. Ch. Kavora Merryborne Sweet Martini, with nineteen CCs.

The record number of CCs won by a black was held by Mr and Mrs Webster's bitch, Sh. Ch. Asquanne's Grainne, who won 36 CCs. This record has recently been overtaken by Penny Lester's Sh. Ch. Quettadene Mystique with 38.

COCKER OF THE YEAR

In 1969, Arnold Hall, then breed correspondent for *Dog World,* introduced the idea of a Cocker of the Year award for the top winning Cocker, based on the number of CCs and Res. CCs won during any one year. This has been maintained annually since, and the overall results have been as follows.

1969 Winner: Mrs J. Caddy's Ch. Ouaine Chieftain. Reserve: Miss P. Trotman's Sh. Ch. Kavora Merryborne Sweet Martini.

1970 Winner: Miss P. Trotman's Sh. Ch. Kavora Merryborne Sweet Martini. Reserve: Mrs J. Caddy's Ch. Ouaine Chieftain.

1971 Winner: Mrs J. Caddy's Ch. Ouaine Chieftain. Reserve: Mrs K. Doxford's Sh. Ch. Broomleaf Blithe Spirit.

1972 Winner: Miss J. Macmillan's Sh. Ch. Lochranza Newsprint. Reserve: Mr G.

Williams' Ch. Bournehouse Starshine.

1973   Winner: Mr G. Williams' Ch. Bournehouse Starshine. Reserve: Mr A. Mansfield's Ch. Lucklena Light Music.

1974   Winner: Miss J. Macmillan's Sh. Ch. Newsreader of Lochranza. Reserve: Mrs J. Chadwick's Sh. Ch. Merryworth Mr Chips.

1975   Winner: Miss J. Macmillan's Sh. Ch. Newsreader of Lochranza. Reserve: Mr G. Williams' Ch. Bournehouse Starshine.

1976   Winner: Mr G. Williams' Ch. Bournehouse Starshine. Reserve: Mrs T. Bebb's Sh. Ch. Ramiro of Ronfil.

1977   Winner: Mrs M. Stevens' Sh. Ch. Raneyl Late Summer of Leabank. Reserve: Mr and Mrs Darby's Sh. Ch. Kenavon Envoy.

1978   Winner: Miss J. Macmillan's Sh. Ch. Lochranza Man of Fashion. Reserve: Mr M. Armstrong's Sh. Ch. Bitcon Silver Model.

1979   Winner: Miss J. Macmillan's Sh. Ch. Lochranza Man of Fashion. Reserve: Miss P. Trotman's Sh. Ch. Kavora Blackbird.

1980: Winner: Mr G. Parkin's Sh. Ch. Bitcon Florin of Mistfall. Reserve: Mrs D. Barney's Sh. Ch. Cilleine Athene.

1981   Winner: Mrs D. Barney's Sh. Ch. Cilleine Echelon. Reserve: Mrs J. Smith's Sh. Ch. Sorbrook Brambleberry.

1982   Winner: Mrs D. Barney's Sh. Ch. Cilleine Echelon. Reserve: Mrs S. Clarke's Sh. Ch. Roanwood Ripple.

1983   Winner: Mrs D. Barney's Sh. Ch. Cilleine Echelon. Reserve: Miss J. Macmillan's Sh. Ch. Lochranza Like Your Style.

1984   Winner: Mrs A. Hackett's Sh. Ch. Lindridge Gypsy Girl. Reserve: Mrs P. Lester's Sh. Ch. Quettadene Emblem.

1985   Winner: Mr H. Jones' Sh. Ch. Matterhorn Montana. Reserve: Mrs P. Lester's Sh. Ch. Quettadene Emblem.

1986   Winner: Mrs P. Bentley's Sh. Ch. Canigou Mr Happy. Reserve: Mrs A. Webster's Sh. Ch. Asquanne's Ghia.

1987   Winner, Miss P. Becker's Sh. Ch. Olanza Poacher's Moon. Reserve: Mrs A. Webster's Sh. Ch. Asquanne's Ghia.

1988   Winner: Miss P. Becker's Sh. Ch. Olanza Poacher's Moon. Reserve: Mrs A. Webster's Sh. Ch. Asquanne's Ghia.

1989   Winner: Mr and Mrs E. Darby's Sh. Ch. Classicway Cutty Sark. Reserve: Mrs A. Hackett's Sh. Ch. Lindridge Vanity Fair.

1990   Winner: Mrs S. Platt's Sh. Ch. Charbonnel Fair Cher. Reserve: Mrs A. Webster's Sh. Ch. Asquanne's Grainne.

1991   Winner: Mrs A. Webster's Sh. Ch. Asquanne's Grainne. Reserve: Mrs S. Platt's Sh. Ch. Charbonnel Fair Cher.

1992   Winner: Mrs A. Webster's Sh. Ch. Asquanne's Grainne. Reserve: Mrs K. Armstrong's Sh. Ch. Bitcon Troubador.

1993   Winner: Mrs P. Lester's Sh. Ch. Quettadene Mystique. Reserve: Mrs P. Bentley's Sh. Ch. Canigou Patent Applied For.

1994   Winner: Mrs P. Lester's Sh. Ch. Quettadene Mystique. Reserve: Mrs P. Bentley's Sh. Ch. Canigou Cambrai.

JUDGING COCKER SPANIELS
Kennel Club Regulations cover all aspects of dog showing and judging. It is required that judges should judge in accordance with the Breed Standard laid down by the Kennel Club. The judge must accept that responsibility; and his knowledge of dogs and of the relevant Breed Standard should be enough to ensure that exhibitors can have complete faith in his ability to judge that particular breed.

REQUIREMENTS FOR A JUDGE
The basic and all-important principle is that all judgments are honestly made. There should be no place for favours for friends, no preconceptions based on what the judge has seen before, and no suggestion of the judge getting his own back for any past failures of his own dogs. The construction, condition and movement of the dog on the day is all that counts – or it should be.

The next prerequisite is a knowledge of construction of dogs in general and the breed in particular, as well as an understanding of how that particular breed propels itself along. For instance, a Cocker Spaniel moves differently from a Chow-Chow. The Breed Standard gives a broad picture, but knowledge of technical terms connected with dogs and a full understanding of them are absolutely essential.

For example, the would-be judge must know what the ideal bend of stifle, or size of leg bone, should be in the breed he is judging. These are points learned over a long period of time, though it is very easy after a couple of years to think you know it all. Time will tell you that you were wrong. You can learn by watching good dogs, and by talking to experienced exhibitors with really good dogs.

Judging is not an exact science and judges are bound to show differences in opinion by their placings. Marginal differences are likely to occur. It is when these placings are too far apart that people begin to question who is right and who is wrong.

In Britain, there are no tests or examinations for judges. Anyone selected by a Show Committee can judge at all but Championship shows. The Kennel Club has to approve judges for Championship Shows at which Challenge Certificates are on offer. The result of this at Open Shows can be that up-and-coming judges are given a better chance of gaining experience. It is, however, more often the case that a judge is asked to judge a number of breeds which he is never likely to judge at a Championship Show.

In approving judges to judge at Championship Shows, the Kennel Club invariably seeks the opinion of Breed Councils or Breed Clubs, but it does reserve the right to make the decision, since the KC has the sole right to allocate Challenge Certificates (CCs) to shows. The advice of the Council or Clubs is usually followed, but not always. The system works well in general, but odd cases do arise where a would-be judge can use influence with friends to secure appointments, while a competent but reticent person is overlooked.

Practically all other countries have national Kennel Club examinations for people wishing to judge. In Finland, I was invited to sit on the panel conducting an oral examination of candidates who had already passed the written examinations. This took the form of each candidate describing in detail what he or she thought of several dogs of varying quality. They had to state whether a particular dog had a good head or a poor head, good shoulders or bad shoulder placement, etc. Panel members used their experience and judgment of the dog to assess the knowledge of each of the candidates in turn. Three of the five candidates were given a 'Pass', but two were told they needed more experience and knowledge of the breed before applying again.

Nevertheless, it is a fact that British judges are very highly thought of throughout the world. When I judged in the USA I was intrigued to receive general advice from the American Kennel Club on judging procedures, which included advice on dress. They expect their judges to look smart. This is good advice. A judge should look his (or her) best, and appear confident. While standards generally are high in Britain, there are some judges who do not present a good picture to onlookers.

BEFORE THE SHOW
Before judging commences, the judge will receive a judging book from the show organisers. He will have to fill this in as he goes along. Normally, one slip will go to the Awards Office, one to the secretary of the show, and one will be placed on a board in the ring showing the awards made in each class. The judge should see that he, or his steward, makes a note of absent dogs. It is a surprising fact that although entry fees are not cheap nowadays, about 30 per cent are usually absent. It is necessary to know these absentee figures when calculating how many dogs a person has judged when the Kennel Club is deciding whether he has enough experience to be a Championship Show judge.

RING PROCEDURE
The judge usually starts with the dogs standing in line, and takes a preliminary, general look at them. Then they are usually sent around the ring, giving the judge a general impression of them as they move, and also giving the dogs a chance to loosen up. Each dog is then seen individually on the table, and the judge uses his hands to examine the dog. I stress the use of his hands. I personally do not think it is possible to see what is under the coat, or how well-muscled a dog is, without handling it. At a comparatively recent show, an overseas judge hardly touched the dogs, and almost all the exhibitors signed a complaint to the Kennel Club about his judging.

It is essential that the examination is done in a kindly but firm and confident way, and that it covers all the points of the dog. Gentle handling is a must, particularly with puppies. Rough handling by a judge can easily put a dog off showing. The dog should be able to enjoy the show as much as his owner.

Having seen a dog on the table, the judge must then assess how well it moves. If a dog is made correctly, it should move correctly. As the dog moves, the front legs should be parallel and so should the back legs. Some American experts say that the quicker a dog moves, the more the legs will converge (i.e. slope inwards towards the feet as speed increases). In my opinion and that of many Cocker judges, a Cocker does not attain sufficient speed while on the lead for that to happen. If the dog does not move steadily enough for the judge to assess movement, the owner should be asked to move the dog again. It is important to watch not only from the front and the back, but from the side as well. The judge can then see the topline of the dog on the move, which should be level, and the drive or power behind the movement. A Cocker should be long-striding. Fast, short steps are not good movement.

MAKING DECISIONS

When all the dogs have been seen and moved, decision time arrives. The judge who dithers is not popular with exhibitors. He should take time to make up his mind, but when he does so he should be firm and decisive. A judge who continually alters placings does not inspire confidence in the exhibitors. The Kennel Club requires that at the end of each class, the winning dogs should be placed in the centre of the ring in descending order from left to right.

After all the classes have been judged, unbeaten exhibits are called for, and the steward usually places them in class order. At Open Shows, this is for the selection of Best of Breed. At Championship Shows, it is for the Challenge Certificate to be awarded. It is important to remember, when the Reserve Challenge Certificate is awarded, that the second in the class of the Challenge Certificate winner is considered.

No discussion or talk with exhibitors is allowed when judging, but it is important that judges are polite and pleasant to exhibitors. Even when it is obvious to the judge that a dog has no chance of winning, that dog must be judged with the same thoroughness as the best. Remember that the owner has paid for that privilege.

WRITTEN REPORTS

At shows in most countries overseas, the judge has to complete a report on each dog. It is always a little difficult to know how critical that report should be. No exhibitor likes to know that the judge finds a great deal wrong with his dog. I sometimes wonder how over-critical reports affect future invitations. However, most exhibitors accept honest, constructive criticism with good grace. In Britain, the judge is asked to submit a report to the dog papers, and that report is usually confined to the good points – rightly or wrongly.

GENERAL ADVICE

Judging can be an enlightening experience. You have to bear in mind that the perfect dog has yet to be born. All have their shortcomings in someone's eyes. All have some good points. The judge must balance the two, without letting his liking for particular points affect his overall judgment. Also remember that, although stewards are usually very helpful, it is the judge who is in charge of the ring.

In 1991, the Kennel Club published a booklet, *Guide for Judges*, which is still available at a cost of 50 pence. This explains what is expected from a judge of dogs at shows of all levels. It recommends that this be read in conjunction with KC Show Regulations. I would recommend anyone who judges, whether for the first time or as a more experienced person, to acquire and read this booklet. It contains much useful advice.

Nowadays, some clubs hold judging seminars, at which people who wish to judge (or maybe wish to learn more about a breed before accepting an invitation to judge it) are instructed by an experienced judge of that breed. Quite often these seminars include hands-on experience, so that verbal instruction is backed up with practical experience of handling a dog. Such seminars are becoming popular and are very worthwhile.

Many judges feel that acting as steward before becoming a judge helped them to gain much-needed experience and knowledge of individual breeds, as well as being educational as far as ring procedure is concerned.

KEEPING RECORDS
For anyone hoping to reach the highest level of judging, at Championship Show level, it is essential that records of all shows judged (the date of the show, name of the Society, whether it was an Open or Limited Show, the number of classes for each breed, the number of dogs of each breed entered, and the number of entries made in each breed, as well as the number of absentees in each breed) be carefully kept. Such information will be required when consideration is given to any application for permission to judge a breed for the first time at a Championship Show.

Chapter Seven

BREEDING AND WHELPING

REASONS FOR BREEDING

When a litter is planned, it is most important for the breeder to know *why* the litter is planned. Puppies should only be produced when there is a very good reason, such as wanting to produce something better than is already owned, or something to follow on from appreciated family lines. To produce puppies just for the purpose of making money is the wrong reason for breeding

BREEDING CONSIDERATIONS

The age at which a bitch should have a first litter is always debatable, but most people prefer not to mate until at least the second season. If that is at an early age, it is better to leave it until her third season. The Cocker Spaniel Council in its *Code of Ethics* recommends that a bitch should not be bred from until she is at least sixteen months of age. The Kennel Club does not have a regulation regarding the minimum age of a bitch, but it will not accept registrations for puppies from a bitch who has already had six litters, or is over the age of eight years.

The next question you should consider is whether you will have the facilities to rear a litter properly, and also the time and patience to cope with a litter. Facilities will be dealt with later in the chapter, but I would emphasise here that producing a litter is a very time-consuming activity, and patience with the puppies when they are growing up is also required.

Nowadays, there are breeders who keep dogs (not only Cockers) just for breeding for profit. Most bona-fide breeders deplore such establishments – usually puppy farmers who mass-produce puppies of popular, commercially viable breeds. In many of these establishments, conditions are not always as good as they should be.

AIMS OF A BREEDER

The aim of a genuine breeder should be to produce top-quality puppies of good type, with happy temperaments. Anything of poor quality or doubtful temperament simply gives ammunition to the anti-dog brigade which is so prevalent today. The Breed Standard says: "Temperament: Gentle and affectionate, yet full of life and exuberance". Let me emphasise that a Cocker Spaniel with a poor temperament, whether it be from aggression, possessiveness, or nervousness, is not a typical Cocker.

Any potential breeder must be sure of finding good homes for those puppies not retained. When puppies go to new homes, it is essential that they should go where they will have a lot of love and affection, as well as good food and housing. Cocker puppies are charming little characters, loved by children in particular, but they should never be sold as children's playthings for they could end up being discarded when interest wanes. Permanent homes should always be aimed for.

Obviously, on rare occasions, circumstances prevent an owner, or family, from keeping the puppy for the rest of its life (such as hospitalisation of a single owner). In these cases, the breeder should always be prepared to take the dog back and keep it until another suitable home can be found. It is all too easy to sit back and say that one of the Rescue Societies can cope with such a situation, but as a breeder you should always be prepared to help where possible.

FITNESS OF THE BITCH

Having decided that all these questions can be answered satisfactorily, the next point on which you should focus attention is the fitness of the bitch to produce puppies. She should have no known hereditary defects, and be sound and healthy. There is little point in breeding from a poor-quality bitch – one cannot expect a stud dog, no matter how good or dominant he may be, to make up for all the bitch's shortcomings. It is also very important to breed only from bitches with good temperament. To perpetuate nervousness and bad or uncertain temperament, even if only to breed from a valued family pet is, in my opinion, totally wrong.

CHOICE OF STUD DOG.

If you decide, after due consideration, to produce a litter, you must give some thought to finding a suitable stud dog to use. The good and bad points of both dog and bitch should be taken into account, as well as their pedigrees. Decisions then have to be made as to whether in-breeding, line-breeding, or outcrossing is to be carried out. For the inexperienced breeder, it may be useful to explain as simply as possible the difference between these.

IN-BREEDING

This is where two closely-related animals are mated together, such as father to daughter, mother to son, or brother to sister. This does have the effect of reproducing the very good points of both animals, but should be carried out only by experienced breeders, as it also has the effect of reproducing the faults, or bad points, of both animals too. It may also reproduce any inherited defects which may be carried as a recessive gene by both parents, even though these defects are not apparent in the parents. In some breeds where there is a very small gene pool (such as a breed which is small numerically, and not yet fully established) there is good reason for using in-breeding, but in my opinion, in a breed like the Cocker with a very wide gene pool available, such in-breeding is not really necessary, or wise. I should also add that it is rarely done in Cockers.

LINE-BREEDING

This is where two related animals, coming from similar family lines (but not as closely related as mentioned above) are mated together.

Many breeders approve of line-breeding (e.g. cousins mated together, sometimes grand-daughter to grandfather, grandson to grandmother, niece to uncle or great-uncle), as this is more likely to produce stock of the same type as the parents, but without the risks taken with in-breeding. I was advised by the late Mr Lloyd (of 'Of Ware' fame), in my early days in Cockers, to line-breed, and it has always stood me in good stead. I would definitely recommend it.

OUTCROSSING

This is mating two unrelated animals. Some breeders will do this, by mating two animals of similar type, but differing bloodlines. However, with no family links, production of puppies of the same type is not necessarily to be expected.

Even line-breeding is no guarantee of improvement in stock – results depend on the gene patterns of the two parents. If faults are found, the stud dog should not be blamed entirely. This is often done, but faults are usually from genes carried on both sides. The construction, not only of sire and dam but also of grandparents and other forebears, can influence the construction of puppies. It is therefore very useful when looking at the parents' pedigrees to have some knowledge of the construction and temperament of the dogs and bitches behind them. Novice breeders for whom this may not be possible would be wise to discuss pedigrees with an experienced breeder, or the stud dog owner.

INFLUENCE ON THE BREED

It is easier for a stud dog to have influence on the breed, because of the fact that he is able to produce far more progeny than a bitch. A few dogs have had considerable influence, and these have been:

My own Int. Ch. Ouaine Chieftain produced three Sh. Chs. at home and several more overseas.

Mrs Schofield's Ch. Scolys Starduster sired two Sh. Chs. and one Champion.

His son, the late Mrs Stevens' Sh. Ch. Leabank Levity, produced four Sh. Chs.

Phyllis Masters' black and white dog, Sh. Ch. Chrisolin Cambiare of Styvechale, was the sire of four Sh. Chs. including the black and white dog, Sh. Ch. Styvechale Serenader. The same owner's blue roan dog, Styvechale Stormcloud, produced three Sh. Chs.

Miss Macmillan and Mrs Gillespie's blue roan dog, Hightrees Sweet Talk of Lochranza, though never shown himself, was widely used, and produced three Sh. Chs., including Sh. Ch. Cilleine Echelon.

Denise Barney's Sh. Ch. Cilleine Echelon sired nine Sh. Chs. and other CC winners.

In solids, there have been a number of dogs producing three or more Sh. Chs.

The top producer must be the black dog Sh. Ch. Quettadene Emblem, with nine Sh. Ch. progeny to his credit.

Next in blacks comes Jacky Marris-Bray's Sh. Ch. Janeacre Night Skipper of Helenwood with seven.

ABOVE: Sh. Ch. Perrytree The Dreamer: Sire of three Show Champions. Owned by Mrs J. Rowland.

TOP RIGHT: Sh. Ch. Kells Clannad: Sire of three Show Champions. Owned by Mrs L. Gilmour-Wood.

Photo: T. Morgan.

ABOVE: Normanview Midnight Runner Of Classicway: Sire of six Show Champions. Owned by Mr and Mrs E. Darby.

Photo: Anne Roslin-Williams.

LEFT: Sh. Ch. Bitcon Pacific Blue: Top sire of 1991 and 1992. Owned by M. Armstrong.

ABOVE: Mistfall Meddler: The breed's current top Show Champion producer. Owned by G. Parkin.

RIGHT: Sh. Ch. Asquannes Gonzales: Top sire 1994. Owned by Mr & Mrs A. Webster.

The late Mrs K. Doxford and Poppy Becker's black dog, Sh. Ch. Broomleaf Bright Memory, sired six Sh. Chs.

Miss Macmillan's Sh. Ch. Lochranza Quettadene Marksman was the sire of five Sh. Chs. Lesley Gilmour Wood's Sh. Ch. Kells Clannad has three Sh. Ch. progeny.

Before his departure for North America, Penny Lester's Quettadene Debonair sired three Sh. Chs.

In the red and golden section, top producer over the last 25 years goes to Mr and Mrs J. Smith's Sunglint of Sorbrook, with seven title holders to his credit.

Liz Buttrick and Mrs J.Taylor's Sh. Ch. Cleavehill Pot of Gold won twelve CCs and sired four Champions, including Sh. Ch. Beligar Rambler, the black dog who won the Dog CC at Crufts in 1994.

Sh. Chs. Brandy Butter of Broomleaf and Butterprint of Broomleaf, both owned by the late Kay Doxford, sired three Sh. Chs. each.

Jacky Rowland's dog Sh. Ch. Perrytree The Dreamer has so far produced three Sh. Chs.

To return to particolours, Mr and Mrs Darby's blue roan dog, Normanview Midnight Runner of Classicway, produced six Sh. Chs.

Mr M. Armstrong's Bitcon kennel has produced fourteen Sh. Chs., including the blue roan dog, Sh. Ch. Bitcon Pacific Blue (nine CCs), who has sired two Sh. Chs. and several CC winners, and was top sire of 1991 and 1992; also Sh. Ch. Bitcon Troubador (25 CCs), who is already the sire of three Sh. Ch. progeny, plus another CC winner in the ring yet to make his title. Also housed in the Bitcon kennel is the blue dog, Mistfall Meddler, a son of Bitcon Silver Rebel (by Ouaine Diogenes, one CC, four Res. CCs). Although not a CC winner himself, Meddler won Best Puppy of the Year in 1984 and has made his mark as a sire of lovely type Cockers, with seven Sh. Chs. to his credit. Mistfall Meddler must be the top Sh. Ch.-producing dog alive today.

Mr and Mrs Webster's Sh. Ch. Asquanne's Gonzales, winner of eleven CCs and Res. in the Group at Belfast in 1991, has sired five of the 1994 CC winners and won *Dog World's* Top Stud Dog of the Year award.

If any records have been left out, I extend apologies – any omissions are not intentional.

CARE OF THE IN-SEASON BITCH

Bitches come into season at periodical intervals, and the time between seasons varies from one bitch to another. It is a common misconception, fostered by references in many books, that bitches come into season every six months. This is usually not the case. It is important to remember that the period of time which elapses between the first and second seasons is usually the timespan between future seasons. In other words, once you know your bitch's cycle, she will normally follow her own established pattern.

In my experience, bitches who come into season for the first time as early as eight months, may go only six, seven, or eight months between seasons. In contrast, those who have a first season at over twelve months of age, are likely to go longer, maybe up to twelve months, between seasons. I mention this as a guideline only for newer owners; experienced breeders will already be aware of the fact that no exact timing can be made.

When the bitch is approaching a season, you will probably notice that she licks herself around the vulva more than usual. She will also begin to swell a little in that region.

If the normal pattern is followed, the next stage will be a blood-stained discharge from the vagina, with further enlargement of the vulva. If your bitch is to be mated, care must be taken to keep her away from other dogs from this point on, until approximately two weeks after mating. You should carefully note the time when you first notice that your bitch is in season, particularly if she is to be mated, in order to calculate the right time to mate her. It is important to adhere to the correct time for mating, when the bitch will be most receptive to the stud dog and most likely to conceive. Do not arrange to use a stud dog at a time or day, say at a weekend, just to suit your own convenience. It may not be the right time for the bitch.

Nowadays, vets can do a blood test on a sample taken from the bitch, to predict the best time for mating. However, many experienced breeders use the layman's method (which I have always found very useful and reliable) of swabbing the bitch with cotton-wool each morning. As long as the discharge is a red colour, it is too early to mate, but when the discharge fades to a very pale, rather wishy-washy pink, that is usually the best time. Some breeders expect their bitches to be ready for mating on the eleventh or twelfth day after first showing colour, but others prefer to wait till the thirteenth day. My own bitches over the years have almost always been ready on the eleventh day – with one exception, who had to be mated on the thirteenth.

When the bitch first shows colour, the owner of the stud dog should be contacted. Do not leave it until the bitch is ready to mate. A mutually convenient time will be arranged, and if all goes well, when the bitch is taken to the dog, a successful mating will take place.

MATING
When mating two Cockers, it is not just a case of letting dog and bitch run loose and mate on their own. This could result in a keen stud dog being over-attentive and a bitch resenting such behaviour, and becoming difficult to mate.

Most stud dog owners prefer to let the dog and bitch get acquainted, which helps the bitch to relax. After a short while, the bitch will normally be held in a standing position, firmly but gently, by holding her head and ears so that she cannot pull away. Sometimes the owner is allowed to hold her, but sometimes a more experienced person from the dog's establishment will do so. The stud dog's owner will usually place a hand under the bitch's body to support her while the stud dog mounts her. After the dog has penetrated the bitch, there follows what is commonly called a 'tie'. This lasts for anything from ten minutes to one hour, during which the dog's genital organ is 'locked' inside the vagina of the bitch. While this is progressing, the dog will usually turn and end up either back to back, or side to side, with the bitch.

All this is perfectly normal, but I, and many experienced breeders, feel it is wise to hold both dog and bitch during the duration of the tie. If not held, either one could move restlessly and cause discomfort to the other, and may even cause damage to either dog or bitch or both.

Normally one mating should be sufficient, particularly if the bitch is taken at the appropriate time. Some breeders prefer to have a bitch mated on a second occasion, perhaps 48 hours after the first one. Usually the stud dog owner will try to meet the wishes of the owner of the bitch.

STUD FEES
When the mating has been successfully completed, the stud fee is payable. This is a fee for service rendered, not necessarily a guarantee of the arrival of puppies. Most stud dog owners do, however, provide a free service on a subsequent season if a bitch fails to conceive.

Stud fees vary, and mainly depend on how much winning the dog has done, or how successful his progeny have been. Years ago the stud fee was regarded as being roughly the same price as one would pay for a pet puppy, but in recent years, stud fees have not kept pace with puppy prices. You should agree on how payment is to be made when the date of the stud service is arranged. Years ago, it was fairly common practice for the stud dog owner to accept the first choice of the litter in lieu of a stud fee. Nowadays, with puppy prices being higher than stud fees, not many breeders would be willing to agree to such an arrangement. If any such arrangement is made, I would strongly recommend that the details of the agreement are put in writing, signed by both parties, and a copy of the agreement kept by both. This avoids any possible unpleasantness, or future misunderstandings.

DOCUMENTATION

When the stud fee is paid, the owner of the dog will provide the bitch's owner with a copy of the dog's pedigree, a stud receipt, and a Kennel Club form on which to apply for Kennel Club registration of the puppies.

The KC form has to be completed by the owner of the dog, giving name and address of the owner, name and KC registration number of the dog, and the date of mating. It is a guarantee to the Kennel Club that the mother of the puppies being registered was in fact mated to the particular dog shown on the form. You should keep this form carefully until the puppies arrive, and use it accordingly. Only the breeder of the puppies is allowed to register them nowadays. The stud dog owner will always be willing to give advice.

NAMING PUPPIES

Choosing names for puppies is always interesting, but for newcomers to breeding it may be necessary to point out that regular breeders have a kennel name, called an affix. They pay the Kennel Club for the right to have the sole use of that word in registering puppies. For example, mine is Ouaine, which has been registered with the Kennel Club since 1953. Names from the pedigrees of the parents may appeal, but the kennel name preceding them should not be used for the puppies unless it is owned by the breeder.

Years ago, the kennel name could be used either before or after the name of the dog, but nowadays it can only be used in front of the name (except for a few old-established kennels which still retain the right to use it after the name) when the puppy is registered. An affix at the end means, in most cases, that the dog was not registered initially by the present owner and that it was added on later, usually when the puppy was transferred. Only if both sire and dam were bred by the new owner can his or her affix be added in front of the name.

PEDIGREES

Novice breeders will often receive help and advice from the stud dog owner on how to prepare pedigrees for the puppies. The pedigree of the stud dog should be written (or preferably typed to avoid errors) on the top half of a blank pedigree form, and the pedigree of the mother of the puppies on the bottom half. Care should be taken to be accurate in spelling or copying names – remember that the pedigrees given out with the puppies may be used to prepare pedigrees for future generations.

CARE OF THE IN-WHELP BITCH

The first question asked by new breeders of a litter is: "How will I know whether the bitch is in whelp?" The answer has to be that there is no hard and fast rule. Most bitches will have a day or two (not more) about four weeks after mating when they become rather choosy about food, and like to be coaxed into eating. If this continues, it may be a sign of something wrong, but a couple of days only should be regarded as a natural occurrence.

Keep a very close eye on your bitch, and watch carefully for small signs. One pointer to being in whelp is that, about ten-twelve days after mating, the bitch's nipples may be slightly pink in colour, and stand out rather more than normal. It is not a foolproof guide, but a small indication that things are progressing well. After about five weeks, the bitch will probably begin to thicken around her waistline, and the hair along the sides of the abdomen may tend to curl outwards. By seven weeks, the outward signs will be more visible, especially if she is carrying a fair-sized litter.

My advice, even if only one or two puppies are there and it may be difficult to be sure that the bitch is in whelp, is to treat your bitch throughout the nine weeks' gestation period as if she *is* in whelp. If she proves not to be pregnant, maybe she will have put on a little excess weight and have to go on a diet afterwards, but this is preferable to cutting her short of all the necessary food and food supplements she will need to carry a litter.

WORMING

Your bitch should be wormed, either just before mating, or within one week afterwards. Some vets recommend worming at regular intervals during pregnancy, but I do not like giving a pregnant bitch worming substances. I prefer to worm my bitches just after mating, and not again until they have finished with the puppies, at around seven or eight weeks after giving birth.

Whatever you decide to do, please ensure that you read carefully the instructions regarding pregnant bitches on any worming mixture or tablets, and follow them just as carefully in administration and dosage.

FEEDING THE BITCH DURING PREGNANCY

Today this is a matter of which type of feeding method the breeder chooses to employ. I confess that I am, in the eyes of some people, old-fashioned as far as feeding goes, but my vet says there is nothing wrong with that. I prefer the tried and trusted method of feeding my dogs, whether pregnant bitches or not, on fresh meat with added wholemeal biscuit meal, rather than the modern system of dry, so-called 'complete' feeds. One reason for this is that the dry feeds cause dogs to drink a lot. I do not consider this good for them, especially if the dog has eaten a large dry feed, as this will then swell up considerably in the dog's stomach, and may cause discomfort. For a bitch in whelp, this could cause even greater discomfort.

However, the type of food to use is a personal decision for the breeder, and the following recommendations are based entirely on my own experience and the results I have had. For any breeder who chooses to use the complete feed method of feeding, I have no advice to offer except to say that you should ensure that you carefully follow the instructions given by the manufacturers.

I must admit that for many people, the complete feed method is very much a labour-saving exercise, and dogs can be left for long periods unattended with food to pick at as and when they choose. I do not think dogs should be able to eat on and off all day. A dog's appetite, good or otherwise, is some indication of whether the dog is well – if he is not, he will refuse food. If food is left down all day for one or more dogs, it is impossible to tell how much or how little a particular dog is eating at any one time, and so the guide to good health is not apparent. Also, if more than one dog is kept under these conditions, you cannot be sure just how much each dog is taking, making it difficult to control the weight of each dog as you can do with the 'old-fashioned' method of feeding. An adult bitch's normal diet consists of a few hard biscuits in the morning, and a main feed of meat (usually raw, sometimes cooked, and occasionally tinned) plus soaked wholemeal biscuit meal, with a vitamin and mineral supplement added.

This diet should be maintained for the first three weeks of pregnancy, but with the addition of extra calcium. Some people believe that giving extra calcium early in pregnancy will make the puppies too large, but I have never found this to be so. It merely gives them the strong bone they should have. I find the easy way to administer the calcium is in the form of palatable calcium tablets, which the dogs like and will take and eat like sweets. Remember that with most calcium or vitamin/mineral products, the recommended dosage varies for small, medium, and large breeds. A Cocker is a medium breed, but the amount of bone it should have is much greater than, for example, another medium breed, the Miniature Poodle. For this reason, I recommend giving a little more calcium than is normally recommended on the package.

After the first three weeks, the bitch should be given two smaller feeds instead of one main feed, with the addition of Vitamins A and D in the form of two cod-liver or halibut-liver oil capsules per day. The Vitamin A is useful in helping the placentas of the litter to adhere to the wall of the uterus. The Vitamin D helps the bitch to absorb the calcium supplements. Continue with these extra vitamins and calcium throughout the pregnancy and until the puppies are completely weaned. When five weeks have elapsed, if the bitch is showing fairly definitely in whelp, the quantity of the two meals should be increased slightly. After the sixth week, the feeds should be given three times a day, and, if increased, should be increased by the addition of more protein rather than carbohydrate. If your bitch is looking heavy in whelp, do not expect her to eat enormous meals, as this would cause her to be uncomfortable. Several small meals are far better.

Occasionally a bitch will, during the last week of pregnancy, develop milk in her glands and if this happens, in order to reduce discomfort and prevent possible suckling problems for the new-born puppies, protein in the diet should be reduced until after whelping.

EXERCISE
It is important for any pregnant bitch to have gentle exercise throughout the nine-week period of carrying the puppies. In the early weeks your bitch may have her normal exercise unless it is very vigorous, but as the pregnancy progresses, she should be allowed to exercise as little or as much as she wishes. She should be discouraged from jumping up on to furniture, and also be protected from other dogs bumping into her. A bitch in good muscular condition will whelp more easily than a fat bitch in slack condition.

PREPARATIONS FOR WHELPING
Prior to the actual whelping, it is very useful to arrange a place where the puppies will be born, but which your bitch can get used to in advance. No bitch likes to be taken from her normal surroundings and thrust into a strange place suddenly at the best of times, and certainly not just prior to whelping.

The majority of breeders nowadays bring their bitches into the house to whelp. This is very convenient, and much more comfortable for the owner, as it is possible to keep an eye on the bitch and see how much progress is being made. I barricade off a portion of my kitchen, with the whelping box in one corner. There is room for the bitch to move around freely in the penned-off area, and I find she quickly settles down and loves being near to me. She is usually installed in her whelping quarters about ten days before the litter is due.

An additional benefit of a litter being born in the house is that as the puppies grow, they become accustomed to normal household noises such as the washing machine, the vacuum cleaner and the radio. This means that when they go to new homes, they are not afraid of such noises.

The whelping box in which the bitch is to have her puppies should be long enough, and wide enough, for her to lie out flat on her side, and still leave room for the pups. It should, of course, be scrupulously clean to prevent any infection of bitch or puppies. I prefer a sectional wooden box which can be dismantled for cleaning and disinfecting after use, in preparation for the next time it is used.

Before whelping, your bitch will appreciate a cosy blanket to lie on, and maybe when whelping is imminent, newspapers to tear and scratch up. I never leave a loose blanket in the bed for the bitch after whelping, as this may be scratched up into folds, and puppies could easily be suffocated or lain on by mistake. I find it best to have a board (plywood or hardboard) about one inch smaller in length and width than the base of the whelping box, which I slot into a pillow-case type covering (made from fleecy fabric) and then tuck the ends under the board. The weight of the bitch anchors it down and she cannot scratch the bedding into folds or ridges.

Giving a firm fabric cover to the board helps to provide a firm footing for the puppies, and they seem to get on their feet much earlier in life than if they are left on newspapers or other smooth surfaces. I prepare several of these board covers in advance, so they can be changed and washed as frequently as necessary.

Heating of some sort should be organised in readiness for whelping. Puppies need warmth, and most normal household central heating systems are switched off at the coldest time, during the night. Also remember that heat rises, and therefore down at floor level it is much cooler than at head height.

For this reason, I strongly recommend an infra-red lamp hung above the whelping box, to provide an even, constant temperature in the base of the box, at around 72 degrees Fahrenheit. Puppies cry mainly for one of two reasons – cold or hunger. By providing constant warmth the first of these problems is overcome. It is possible to obtain infra-red heaters in the form of bulbs, or dull-emitters. I prefer the red-coloured bulb, as the white ones give off a very bright light which is rather hard on the eyes of the bitch. The dull-emitters are equally good for warmth, but I find that the bitch likes the light from the lamp overnight – it helps her to see what is happening to her babies!

The heater should be hung, if possible, towards one end of the box to enable the bitch to move alway from the direct heat if she wishes. You will notice how the puppies tend to go to the warmer end.Another form of heating available is the electric heating pad, which is placed underneath the bedding in the whelping box. I have seen one of these used with another breed quite successfully, but as my bitches like to scratch up any loose bedding, I feel these heating pads would not be suitable for them.

Other things to have ready in preparation for the whelping are:

1) A good supply of newspapers.
2) Plenty of old towels.
3) A cardboard box containing a rubber hot-water bottle, and a piece of cosy blanket (I recommend 'Vetbed', an acrylic-type fleecy fabric with a firm backing).
4) A pair of sterilised scissors.
5) Disinfectant such as Dettol.
6) Cotton wool and a roll of kitchen paper.
7) A bowl for warm water and a small flannel or face cloth.
8) A notepad and pen to keep records
9) A milk substitute made especially for puppies, or a full cream baby milk.
10) A Belcroy feeder, to which I will refer later.

Before whelping becomes imminent, get the bitch used to having her temperature taken. To do this, use either a stubby-ended human thermometer, or one of the easier to read battery-operated digital thermometers now available. The normal temperature of a dog is 101.5 degrees F.

Take your bitch's temperature (by gently inserting the thermometer into the rectum) each morning and evening for a week before the puppies are due. The normal pattern is for the temperature to go down gradually. When it reaches 99 degrees or less, it means that whelping is imminent and the puppies will usually arrive within 24 hours. This is a very good guide, though not a precise timing. If you record temperatures when you take them, you can provide reliable information for the vet, should he be needed. It also helps the owner to be prepared mentally as well as physically for the event.

One other thing which you can do to ensure puppies as free from problems as possible is to bathe the bitch's milk glands very gently with warm water daily during the week before whelping. This ensures that the puppies are feeding from clean milk vessels. The milk glands should be dried off with a soft towel after bathing.

Your vet should be advised at least a week ahead of the date that a litter is expected, and asked if he will be available if needed. This will ensure that if he is needed in an emergency, he is aware of the reason and will respond quickly to any calls you may have to make. Do not leave it until the whelping is taking place before contacting him: this is unfair to the vet – and to your bitch, as it may cause undue delay. Most vets are very co-operative with considerate clients, and building up a good relationship is of paramount importance and will stand you in good stead as the years go by.

IMMINENT SIGNS OF WHELPING
As whelping approaches, during the preceding 24 hours or so, many bitches will have refused food, though others may eat up until the whelping process actually starts.

Most bitches will lick themselves frequently around the vulva, which will be somewhat swollen and soft. If there is to be a large litter, there is often a *clear* mucous discharge. If the discharge is a dirty dark brown or green colour, it is a sign of something wrong (maybe a dead puppy) and veterinary advice should be sought immediately. If the discharge is clear and colourless, it is perfectly normal.

Frequent passing of urine and faeces in small quantities is normal for 24 hours or so before whelping. Newspaper put in the whelping box for the bitch to scratch up helps her to prepare for her puppies' arrival. Sometimes your bitch will vomit, particularly after she has taken a drink of water. As the birth draws closer, the bitch will sit and shiver, and you will possibly see slight strains. These are the early signs that labour is commencing.

THE WHELPING

It is a good idea to write down the time at which straining is first noticed so that, should problems arise, the vet can be given accurate information. Such information can be crucial in times of difficulty.

When quite strong straining is evident, the first stage of the water bag appearing should follow within an hour. The actual bag may not itself be seen, but a sudden rush of fluid will keep your bitch occupied, licking it up rapidly. She may rest for a short while, then straining will recommence. Within an hour, vigorous straining will be apparent, which should result in the birth of the first puppy.

Throughout this period, most bitches like to have their owners present, even if only for words of comfort and sympathy. Bear in mind that most bitches whelp during the night, so you should be prepared for staying up with your bitch for one night, if not more.

Most Cocker bitches when whelping for the first time will cry out when the first puppy is arriving. This is partly from a little fear of what is happening, and partly from any labour pains they may feel. They rely on their owner to give them some sympathetic and encouraging words as they go on. After the first puppy, the others usually arrive without the bitch being unduly worried.

Puppies are normally born in a sac of fluid, and arrive head first with their nose on the front paws. Attached to the sac is the umbilical cord, and the placenta (or afterbirth). It is usual for the bitch to tear open the sac immediately, sever the cord without damaging the puppy, and then eat up the afterbirth which is a dark greenish colour. She will proceed to lick the puppy all over, cleaning it and drying it.

If she does not do this, either from inexperience or lack of maternal instinct (which I must say is rare in a Cocker), you must act quickly. Tear open the bag – the best place to do this is at the end near the puppy's nose – and remove it from around the puppy. The cord should be attended to. Some people believe it should be cut with sterilised scissors and tied with thread, but a vet friend advised me many years ago that by doing that, the bitch is not encouraged to deal with the procedure herself. He recommended that the cord be broken off about three inches from the puppy's navel (but by pulling the cord away from the placenta towards the puppy, not away from the puppy, to avoid causing an umbilical hernia), then tied in a knot to prevent bleeding from the puppy. If it is then given to the bitch, she will usually lick it, and finally get the message of how to sever the cord near to the puppy, and know how to cope with the following puppies herself. On the rare occasions that I have had to deal with a puppy, this advice has worked.

If the bitch does not lick and dry the puppy, take a towel and gently rub the pup all over to remove surface fluids, and then hand it back to the bitch for her to complete the process. Most bitches do not like undue interference, so avoid this if all is progressing well.

After the birth of the first puppy the mother will settle down and her puppy may suckle straightaway. If another puppy is on the way fairly quickly, the bitch may not want the puppy to suckle for a while. I always have on hand a jar of runny honey, and give each puppy a small amount by dipping my little finger into the jar and then putting my finger into the puppy's mouth. Honey is a natural substance, cannot do the puppy or its digestion any harm, and tends to keep the puppy contented until it can feed from its mother. Also, when the puppy sucks at my finger to get the honey, I know whether it has strong suction – which means that it will be able to hold on to a nipple strongly when feeding from its mother. All this is done while the puppy is still in the whelping box, as it would probably distress the bitch to take the puppy away. If the bitch licks some honey from around the puppy's mouth, it will do her no harm.

Some puppies are born backwards, known as a breech birth. Provided they are still enclosed in the sac, this does not usually cause problems. However, if the sac breaks before the puppy is born, the small claws on the puppy's hind feet can be somewhat painful for the bitch. A sudden rush of fluid into the pup's mouth can sometimes result in it being drowned, or fluid being taken into the lungs. Either of these eventualities can present a problem.

If your bitch has any difficulty in passing a puppy, whether from a normal presentation or a breech birth, you can help by holding with a towel the part of the puppy protruding from the vagina, and gently easing the puppy out downwards *as the bitch strains*. No undue pulling or tugging should be done, as this can damage both bitch and puppy.

As whelping progresses, make a note of the time of arrival of each puppy. Again, this provides useful information in case of difficulties. I also make a note of the sex of each puppy, and with particolours it is interesting to note down the markings of each puppy for easy identification later. Even with solid colours, there are often a few white hairs visible to distinguish one pup from another.

The time between the arrival of one puppy and the next can vary considerably, but *if the bitch is straining strongly* and no puppy arrives, she should not be allowed to go on for more than an hour before you call the vet. To leave your bitch for longer is to risk her being over-exhausted before whelping is completed.

I find that by using newspapers during the whelping, I can simply place more clean ones on top of soiled ones until the bitch has finished. Afterwards they can all be removed and a cosy covering on the base-board (as described earlier) can be put in the whelping box.

If a large litter is being born, the bitch may like to have a drink of milk between the arrival of one puppy and the next. After they are born, all puppies should be encouraged to suckle from their mother, as this action stimulates the uterus and helps to bring the other puppies down. If the puppies arrive very quickly one after another, there may not be

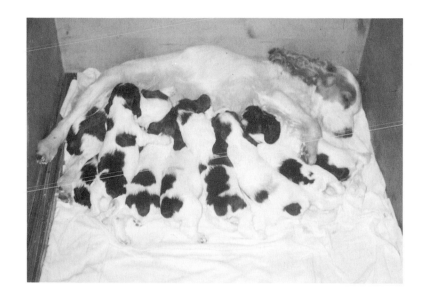

Cocker Spaniels generally make good mothers: This bitch is caring for a litter of nine puppies.

time for the mother to keep them all dry and to deal with the next birth. If this happens, all but the last one born may be gently removed from the whelping box and placed on a hot-water bottle wrapped in a towel, which gives off gentle heat, until the mother has coped with the new arrival.

If any of this distresses the bitch, it may be possible to place the wrapped hot-water bottle in a corner of the whelping box and place the puppies on to it until the bitch can cope with them all.

Cockers are comparatively easy whelpers, and if all goes well, both mother and puppies should be lying contentedly in a warm and cosy bed within a few hours. Puppies will suckle frequently, and your bitch will be continuously washing their faces and cleaning them up when they pass urine and faeces. This is normal, and keeps the bitch busily occupied.

She should be disturbed as little as possible, but may have to be encouraged to go outside to relieve herself occasionally, as she will not want to leave her babies. As long as the puppies are contented and not crying, things should progress well.

CRYING PUPPIES

This is a sign of something wrong. It may be that the mother does not have sufficient milk, or that the puppies are not sucking strongly enough. If for any other reason, seek veterinary advice quickly, as infection may be the cause, and infection in newborn puppies can be fatal.

The milk supply of the mother can be stimulated by giving frequent drinks of warm milk. If it becomes necessary to supplement the feeding of the puppies, products are available which closely resemble bitches' milk, and can also be used for weaning later.

Many years ago the late Judy de Casembroot of the famous Treetops Cockers told me about a premature human baby feeding bottle called a Belcroy Feeder. It is made by John

Bell and Croyden of Wigmore Street, London. It is inexpensive, and a tremendous help if puppies need to be fed by the owner, either because they are orphans, or because they need some supplementary feeding. It is a tubular glass bottle with a narrow neck and a small teat at one end, and a valve at the other, wider end.

If a puppy is able to suck well, you can use the Belcroy like any baby's bottle. However, if for any reason the puppy does not have the strength to suck, the valve at the end can be touched very gently and a drop of the milk mixture will fall into the puppy's mouth. It should not be pressed heavily, or too much milk will rush out and the puppy may choke. Spare teats and valves can be obtained from the manufacturer. Before any milk substitute is put into the bottle it should be strained to remove lumps – the hole in the teat is very small and clogs easily.

I would not have a bitch whelping without my Belcroy at hand. Fortunately, I have seldom needed to use it, but on those occasions it has proved invaluable. It has been loaned out to friends from time to time as a standby, and everyone has been favourably impressed.

WEIGHING PUPPIES
Puppies can lose condition very rapidly if they fail to feed properly, and weight lost during the first 48 hours is extremely difficult to pull back. Weigh all puppies shortly after birth, and keep a record of these. I weigh all my puppies daily, writing the weights down, so that I can be sure all are progressing well. Any weight loss – for example one small puppy in a large litter may get pushed out by the larger greedier ones – can be attended to by giving supplementary feeding until the puppy is able to fend for itself.

Average Cocker puppies, if sturdy and well boned (as they should be if the mother has been given all the right food and nutrients during pregnancy) are born between eight and twelve ounces each. They should progress gradually and regularly until they reach about five pounds in weight at about six weeks of age.

Chapter Eight

REARING A LITTER

CARE OF THE BITCH

For the first 48 hours after whelping, your bitch should be kept on a very light diet of powdered milk feeds thickened with unsweetened cereal to give a little more bulk.

By the third day, she can be given chicken or fish (both boneless, of course) with rice or cereal, as well as the milky feeds. After four days, meat can be given. Raw beef is one of the finest milk-producing foods a bitch can have, but milk feeds must be continued.

If the litter is large, your bitch will naturally need more than if she has only one or two puppies, and discretion should be used. With an average-sized litter of four or five puppies, the bitch will need at least four feeds per day, two of meat and a little cereal, and two milk feeds. Fresh water must also be available at all times, as plenty of fluids help your bitch to produce milk for her family.

The bitch's milk glands should never be allowed to become distended or hard, and overloaded with milk. This causes distress and discomfort for the bitch and difficulty in feeding for the puppies. Run your hand gently over the area each day to see if all feels well. If the glands seem to be filling up too much, the quantity of milk feeds and the amount of raw meat should be reduced accordingly, and increased again when the puppies get a bit older and need more from mother. Normally, there should be no problem unless there are only one or two puppies, and the bitch is over-producing milk. But regulating the intake of fluid and food should counteract any problem.

POST-NATAL TEMPERATURE

After whelping, take your bitch's temperature for at least a week, at least once a day. It will usually be back around 101.5 F, but if it rises to 102.5 F or higher, seek veterinary advice as it may be caused by a uterine infection or a retained placenta. This in turn can affect the puppies through the bitch's milk supply, so professional help is needed. A course of antibiotics will probably be given, and the temperature will soon return to normal.

Your bitch will probably have a discharge for a week or so after whelping, but provided it is not dark green or bright reddish-brown, all should be well. If it is highly coloured, again ask for veterinary advice. Many breeders like to have their vet visit and check the bitch over after whelping, and this is a good thing. However, in this day and age many vets (particularly from city practices) will not make house-calls. If this is the case, and provided all appears to be normal and the bitch is contented, taking her to the surgery for a check-up is of debatable value. The risk of picking up infection from other animals could be greater than one would like to take. If this proves to be the only way and help is needed, an appointment should be made outside of surgery hours if possible.

CARE OF THE NEW LITTER

Under normal circumstances, your bitch will be contented with her new family, and the puppies will thrive. The pups should not be handled except when changing the bedding, and then very gently. Strangers and friends should be discouraged from visiting the puppies, as the bitch will need peace and quiet to get on with her job of feeding and cleaning them.

Until the puppies are properly on their feet, children in the family should not be allowed to handle them, and then only gentle handling should be permitted. It is distressing for the new mother when her puppies are frequently handled, even by someone she knows and loves. Too much interference and handling of puppies has been known to cause a sensitive bitch to take the attitude of "Well, if you want to do it, *you* get on with it", and refuse to look after them herself.

DOCKING

The Breed Standard says "Tails customarily docked". Cockers have been docked for many years by all but a few breeders who object to the practice of docking. Most puppies were docked either by experienced breeders themselves, or by vets, usually at three or four days of age.

In July 1993 a new law came into force in Britain whereby *only veterinary surgeons* are allowed to dock. It is still legal for them to do so. However, following a recommendation against docking from their governing body, the Royal Veterinary College, many will not now do so.

Before mating a bitch, the owner should check with the veterinary practice he or she uses to see if docking will be done. Most people buying a Cocker expect it to be docked. If not, you have to decide whether the bitch should be mated, whether to consult another vet, or whether to have long-tailed puppies. There are vets in most areas who will dock, but it may be necessary to ask around to find one.

The Council for Docked Breeds has done a great deal of good work to retain the right of breeders to have their puppies docked, and has tried to locate practising vets who will co-operate with breeders. Members of the CDB can give help in finding a vet who will dock if necessary. One of the joint honorary secretaries, Mrs. A. Moore, of Sprogmore Kennels, Alesford, Colchester, Essex, is herself a Cocker breeder, and will be happy to supply details of membership of the CDB upon request.

Even though this change in the law caused some worries at the time it came into force, there has in effect been little change in the number of docked Cockers being shown. Only a very small number enter the show ring with long tails. It is not the purpose of this book to argue the pros and cons of docking. It is sufficient to say that I do not consider it to be harmful in any way, or distressing for the puppies, when it is done correctly at a few days old. On the contrary, anyone having seen a Cocker working in heavy undergrowth on the scent of game, wagging its tail furiously to indicate that it is close to flushing the game, will appreciate that a long tail would be detrimental to the dog under those circumstances. I know that not all Cockers actually work in those conditions, but many pet Cockers are taken for walks in woodland where they may hunt around for scents, and even there they could be handicapped by a long tail covered in burrs, and such like.

DEW CLAWS

Cockers are usually born with dew claws on the front legs, and very occasionally on the hind legs too. These are usually removed at the same time as the puppies are docked. However, to clarify a point, I should add that it is still legal for a layman (other than a veterinary surgeon) to remove dew claws. In practice, I think most vets who dock will also remove dew claws at the same time.

NAILS

Puppies' nails should be cut by removing the small curved ends with a pair of nail scissors at about ten days of age, and weekly thereafter to prevent the bitch's glands from being scratched. It is surprising just how quickly pups' nails grow.

EYES

Puppies' eyes will open at about twelve to fourteen days. The bitch will normally keep them clean until that time by her constant washing, but if not, and if any swelling or sticky discharge appears around the eyes, they should be bathed very gently with cotton wool soaked in warm water, then gently dried off. The mother will most probably take over at that point.

PUPPIES FROM THREE TO EIGHT WEEKS
HOUSE TRAINING

Puppies are naturally clean and do not like to soil their bedding, so when they are firmly on their feet and can walk out of the box, the board on the front should be removed to allow them to do so. Newspapers should be placed on the floor in front of the box, and the puppies will quickly learn to come out to relieve themselves. This is good training for them, as when they go to new homes, newspapers can be put down as an aid to house-training. Of course, the newspapers will get soiled quickly and will need changing frequently, especially if it is a large litter.

WEANING

The age at which puppies start to be weaned varies between breeders, and to some extent on how devoted a mother the bitch is, as well as depending on the size of the litter. In my opinion, if the litter is very small (two or three puppies) and the mother is well, and happy to go on feeding them, the puppies may safely be left until three to three and a half weeks of age before weaning begins. With a litter of six or seven, I would start weaning at two and a half to three weeks.

The routine I use is as follows.

First day at midday: Each puppy is given about a quarter of a teaspoon of raw scraped beef. (To prepare this, take a slice of good-quality beef, and scrape it with the edge of a spoon. This will remove the soft portion of the beef in the form of almost a paste, and leave the fibrous part behind. The remainder can be frozen and later minced and used when the puppies are older.) Puppies usually do not need to be taught how to eat this – they love it.

Second day at midday: Each puppy is individually fed so that I know how much each one takes and whether it is a slow or greedy feeder. Each puppy is offered about one tablespoonful of milk mixture (puppy or human baby version) in a very small dish (an ashtray is ideal).

Early evening: One quarter-teaspoon of scraped raw beef.

Third day:
8.00am One quarter-teaspoon scraped raw beef.
1.00pm One tablespoon of milk mixture.
8.00pm.One quarter-teaspoon scraped raw beef.

Fourth day:
8.00am One quarter-teaspoon scraped raw beef.
1.00pm One tablespoon milk mixture.
6.00pm One quarter-teaspoon scraped raw beef.
10.00pmOne tablespoon milk mixture.

Once this routine of four feeds a day is established, it should be continued, with quantities being increased gradually but regularly, until the puppies are eating well.

As the puppies grow, at about four and a half weeks of age, I add a little baby cereal to the milk mixture. This may be fairly expensive, but the puppies enjoy it and thrive on it. At this age, I start to give a very small quantity of a vitamin/mineral supplement to each puppy once a day with the raw meat to produce strong bone and teeth. All supplements should be used strictly according to instructions. Liquid calcium is also added to the milk feed once a day at this point. This can be obtained from good pet stores, or from vets .

At about six weeks of age a fine grade of wholemeal puppy meal (soaked with hot water and left to cool and swell) may be added to the meat feeds. Ordinary unsweetened breakfast cereal may be substituted for the baby cereal, but any changes should be gradual to avoid tummy upsets. At this age, additional calcium can be given in the form of part of

The time to start weaning depends on the size of the litter, and the mother's milk supply.

As the puppies get bigger, they will be keen to explore their surroundings.

a palatable calcium tablet. By this time, the quantities would be about a quarter of a pint of milk and baby cereal twice a day, and two meat feeds of about three ounces each with a little meal added. From five weeks onwards, your bitch will be wanting to get away from the puppies for a while. It is unkind to leave her shut in with them all the time, as by that age they have teeth which are very sharp. She should always be able to come and go as she pleases from now on, and get away from them when she feels like it. The puppies will still try to suckle from her, even if she has less milk – and many bitches will stand for the puppies to try and feed.

After six weeks, she should be encouraged to leave them for longer periods and by eight weeks, the puppies should be completely weaned before they are offered to new homes. By this age they should be getting about one third of a pint of milky food twice a day, and about four ounces of meat and two ounces of meal (weighed wet) at each of two feeds.

VARIATION IN PUPPY DIET
Some variety can be introduced by using cooked meat instead of raw, and sometimes chicken or scrambled egg, but be careful not to make any drastic changes. The meat should always be finely chopped or minced (I find extra-fine, extra-lean frozen beef very good) but if frozen meat is used, it must be very thoroughly thawed before use. A little tinned meat should also be introduced. By giving some variety in the diet, you ensure that when the puppies go to new homes they will be ready to eat the food prepared by their new owners, even if it is not quite like Mum made!

WORMING
Most puppies have roundworms and should be treated for them. If a puppy is heavily infested with roundworms, its coat will be tufty and not lie flat and sleek as a puppy's coat should. There are many proprietary worming preparations on the market suitable for puppies from the age of three weeks onwards. Great care should be taken not to overdose

It is a good idea to introduce some variety into the puppies' diet before they leave for their new homes.

The responsible breeder must be ready to give help and support to owners as the puppies settle into their new homes.

Cocker Spaniel puppies go through markedly different phases as they progress towards maturity. This eight-week-old puppy is owned by Marisa de Elorza in Spain.

At three and a half months, this 'whiskery' pup, called Elliott, has plenty of appeal, but bears little resemblance to the glamorous adult Cocker.
Photo courtesy: Marisa de Elorza.

Elliott pictured at eighteen months, now known as Sp. Ch. Yearling Phardante.

Photo courtesy: Marisa de Elorza.

baby puppies. For the first worming at about four weeks of age, I use a human children's worming syrup, which is obtainable from good chemists and should be given in the dosage of two and a half millilitres per five pounds of body weight (or half a ml per pound body weight of the puppy). Choose a preparation which will be very gentle and safe for young puppies, yet also very effective.

For the second worming at about six weeks of age, I use a roundworm tablet, obtained from my vet, which is given in the dosage of one tablet for each ten pounds of body weight (part tablets can be given in proportion to the weight of the puppy).

For the third worming at eight weeks, I use a worming liquid, obtainable only from the vet. Puppies with worms do not thrive as they should, but if they are treated as suggested above, they should not need treating again until after their inoculation has been completed at about fourteen weeks of age. Your bitch should also be wormed when the puppies are about six weeks of age. If she is one of those bitches who insist on vomiting food for their puppies, you must take care to keep her away from them and prevent her from doing this after worming. The puppies must *not* get her worming dose! She should be wormed again when the puppies are eight weeks old, by which time she should be back on a normal diet.

CHOOSING A HOME-BRED PUPPY
If you are planning to keep a puppy for showing, the best age to make your choice is at about eight weeks, although some breeders prefer to wait until nine weeks, and others until ten weeks. I have found that at eight weeks, the puppies are miniatures of what they will be as adults, and so you can make a reasonable prediction regarding future development.

The puppies should be evaluated carefully, with the help of the stud dog owner or an experienced breeder if necessary. Account should be taken of bone and substance, overall construction and balance, eye and expression, mouth and dentition, feet, and character. A shy puppy is not recommended. Markings on parti-coloured puppies should not influence the decision – a good judge should be able to see beyond markings – and sentiment should not be allowed to affect the choice. Movement can be taken into account, but only when the puppy is moving steadily. Good construction must come before good movement, but if a puppy is made right, it will move right. When making a choice of puppies, it is all too easy for the novice to regard all the puppies as perfect specimens, and to look at them through rose-coloured spectacles. However, it is very unwise to sell puppies as future show winners (or show puppies, as they are sometimes called), because once the puppy has left the breeder, no control can be exercised over the development of the puppy. If the new owner does not rear the puppy as well as the breeder would have done, for example – the puppy may not be given the correct diet, it may be over-exercised at an early age, or it may receive a fright which might affect its confidence – then the puppy will not end up as a show specimen. No guarantee can, or should be given.

LEAVING HOME

When puppies go to new homes they should be accompanied by a diet sheet or feeding chart showing what food and what quantity of food the puppy is used to. This is very important for the well-being of the puppy. Any changes in diet must be gradual, even at this age, otherwise tummy upsets can follow. It is not easy for a new owner when house-training the puppy, or for the puppy itself, if it has diarrhoea or loose motions.

The feeding chart that I give with my puppies shows:

a) Present feeding pattern and diet, together with quantities.

b) The age at which changes can be made: namely, reduce to three meals per day at four months of age, but of course with an increase in the amount given, continuing to increase gradually as the puppy grows; reduce to two meals at six months of age, again with a small increase in quantity of these two. By twelve months of age, a few biscuits in the morning and a main feed in the evening is sufficient.

I also give advice on such things as: house-training; always seeing that clean fresh water is available at all times for the puppy to drink as he wishes; never feeding rabbit or chicken bones or any bones which will splinter (if bones are given they should always be pieces of marrow bone sawn, not chopped, by the butcher); how and when to give rewards and what type.

Breeders usually make recommendations about inoculations, and advise owners that the puppy should be kept away from other dogs and places where other dogs go, until the inoculation programme has been completed.

It is important to remember that, although you may be a person experienced with dogs, some of the new owners may be having a dog for the first time. Others may be having a puppy for the first time in fifteen years or so, and have possibly forgotten how to deal with a little one.

Finally, my chart for new owners says that if anyone has any problems he/she should not hesitate to telephone, as advice and help will always be willingly given. Most new owners really appreciate support such as this, and I always feel that if the new owner is happy with the puppy, the puppy stands a really good chance of being happy with the new owner – which is as it should be.

Chapter Nine

HEALTH AND WELFARE

VETERINARY SURGEONS
As I have stressed throughout this book, a good relationship with your veterinary surgeon is invaluable, and you should always follow his advice. Try to stay with one practice – do not chop and change frequently.

Since moving to the West of England eighteen years ago, I have been a client of the same practice, with two vets, until one retired, and now with only a single practitioner. I have always had a preference for a practice with only one or two vets, because it gives continuity, and they get to know my dogs.

This may not be possible for city dwellers who may have to use a practice with several members of staff. If this is the case, it is wise to ask for the same person if possible on each visit, except in cases of emergency where help is urgently needed and the first available vet will come along. A few things, such as First Aid, can be done by the owner, so do not contact the vet unnecessarily. Remember that to call out a very busy person for something minor may take up valuable time and cause him to be delayed for an emergency elsewhere. On the other hand, *if in doubt or if the dog is distressed,* do not hesitate to seek professional advice. If the condition is serious, delay may make matters worse.

FIRST AID
Cockers as a breed are healthy, with few problems. However, with dogs as with humans, small things crop up, and for this reason I suggest you keep a first-aid kit, which should contain:

Cotton wool.
Lint.
Bandages, stretch and straight.
A bottle of antiseptic lotion.
Arnica lotion for sprains and bruises.
A tube of eye ointment.
A bottle of ear-cleaning fluid.
A pot of coagulating powder or potassium permanganate crystals.

A thermometer, either a human stubby-ended one or a modern digital battery-operated model, which is easier to read.
Small and large syringes (without needles) which make giving medicines easy.
A packet of glycerine suppositories, child's size.
A bottle of liquid paraffin.

A dog's temperature is a good guide to general health. If your dog is off-colour, you may wish to take its temperature. This is done by inserting the thermometer gently into the rectum, and holding it tilted down slightly so that its end touches the wall of the rectum. Hold it there for about a minute in the case of the stubby-ended type, or until it bleeps if it is the digital type. Most dogs do not mind this procedure, but if the dog is restive, get someone to hold him gently but firmly while you take the temperature. The normal temperature of a dog is 101.5 degrees Fahrenheit.

Cut pads can be cleaned with cotton wool soaked in clean warm water, then dried off with more cotton wool. Stop any bleeding, firstly by applying pressure to the wound, and then by application of coagulating powder or permanganate of potash crystals (obtainable from a chemist). Serious or deep cuts should, however, merely be cleaned, and a fresh pad of lint and cotton wool applied to prevent further bleeding. Then seek veterinary advice. On an open wound, permanganate crystals might cause some pain or burning. If toenails are trimmed and the quick is cut, causing bleeding, the same things can be used to stop the flow of blood.

Treat bruises or sprains with arnica lotion, and make the dog rest. If no improvement is seen within 48 hours, or if the dog is in pain in the meantime, get veterinary assistance.

EYE PROBLEMS
If your dog's eyes water occasionally – maybe from exposure to dust or strong winds – apply a little general eye ointment to soothe the eyes. Bear in mind, however, that the dog's eyes can be a clear indication of its health. If the white of the eye is bloodshot, this can indicate something as simple as an upset stomach, or it may be a symptom of something more serious. Keep a check, and take the dog's temperature. If it is normal and stays normal, then it may be nothing alarming. If the temperature is raised, it may be a symptom of infection, and needs veterinary attention. If the white of the eye takes on a yellowish, jaundiced tinge, get veterinary help immediately.

ENTROPION: This is a condition where the eyelids turn in, and the lashes rub against the eye. It is a painful for the dog, causing the eye to water and some excessive blinking. If this is seen in a baby puppy, it may correct itself as the pup grows, but will not necessarily do so. Surgery can be performed to turn the eyelid away from the eye itself.

ECTROPION: This is a condition where the lower eyelid is too slack and causes exposure of the third eyelid. It can lead to infection caused by dust particles, and may cause conjunctivitis. Severe ectropion can be corrected by surgery which lifts and shortens the eyelids.

Both these operations are against Kennel Club regulations and dogs so treated should not be shown. However, if either of these conditions exists, it is kinder for the dog if the operation is carried out.

DISTICHIASIS: This condition appears as a double, or an extra, row of eyelashes. Extra hairs appear at the edge of the eyelid and rub against the surface of the eye. The degree of discomfort felt by the dog depends on how many hairs touch the eye, and the effect varies from mild irritation to ulceration of the eye. Surgery may be able to remove the offending hair roots permanently, though it is a tricky operation. If the dog will co-operate and keep very still, it may be possible for the offending hairs to be plucked out – but they will of course re-grow. Such a surgical operation would be against Kennel Club regulations.

EARS: It is a common misconception that all Cockers have ear problems. This is certainly not true, but Cocker owners can do quite a lot to help to avoid them.

Firstly, the hair around the ear openings should be kept short, so that air can circulate around the ear passages. Secondly, when bathing the dog, as explained in Chapter Five, the ears should be plugged to prevent water getting into the deep passages. If water does enter, it will cause irritation, the dog will scratch, inflammation will set in, and the dog will scratch more, creating a vicious circle. It is better to avoid this is the first place.

When grooming, check the ears about once a week by very gently inserting a small piece of cotton wool. Do not poke deeply or prod into the ears, as they are very sensitive. If the cotton wool is dirty, the ear can be cleaned with a cleaning solution, obtainable from your vet or a good pet store. If the ears continue to be dirty, a few ear drops may be used, but always follow instructions carefully, and seek veterinary advice if trouble persists.

TEETH: Normally no problems occur with young dogs, and provided they are given some hard biscuits to chew on, the teeth and gums will stay healthy. Old dogs, however, may develop tartar, particularly if they have the odd decayed tooth and they decline to eat hard biscuits. Should this happen, your vet can help by giving the dog a general anaesthetic, removing any bad teeth, and scaling the rest. There does not appear to be any rhyme or reason as to why some dogs, fed and cared for in exactly the same way as others, should have problems and others do not, but it does happen sometimes.

GUMS: Gums should be a deep pink colour. They can be an indication of the health of the dog. If they lose colour and become very pale, it may mean something seriously wrong, as can gums turning yellowish. Veterinary advice should be sought immediately. When puppies are changing teeth at about four months, the gums are sometimes sore and swollen. If this happens, soft food only for a few days will overcome any problems.

DIARRHOEA: Faeces can be indicative of good health or otherwise. They should normally be firm and passed without difficulty. If your dog has diarrhoea, it could be caused by a simple thing like the dog having eaten something which did not agree with him, but it can also be a symptom of something more serious. Take your dog's temperature, and if it is normal and stays normal, simple steps can be taken to tighten the bowels. The first is to withhold red meat and/or milk; the second would be to administer kaolin and morphine (as used by humans, but give it as a child's dose); if this is not available, most households have cornflour in the cupboard – about a tablespoonful mixed to a smooth paste with cold water and given to the dog (easiest via the large syringe, without a needle) will do no harm and may help to tighten the bowels. Change the diet temporarily, substituting boiled white rice with chicken for the normal food for about forty-eight hours. Avoid anything with liver in it, as this loosens the bowels. *But*, should the temperature be raised, or if there are blood streaks in the diarrhoea, seek veterinary advice immediately, as either or both of these can be symptoms of some other serious condition such as an infectious disease such as parvovirus or enteritis.

Parvo virus is a serious, usually fatal, disease of young dogs. The symptoms are severe depression, vomiting and profuse, watery, foul-smelling diarrhoea, often with blood. It rapidly leads to collapse and death, due to shock and dehydration. In very young puppies parvovirus attacks the heart muscle causing symptoms of rapid breathing, exercise intolerance and cyanosis (lips and tongue turning blue).

CONSTIPATION: Dogs do not normally have problems with this, but sometimes they will lick all the marrow out of a large bone, and this may have a binding effect on the bowels. About a dessertspoonful of liquid paraffin (or olive oil if no paraffin is available) given by mouth, will quickly go through the dog and may help him to pass a motion without difficulty. If the dog is concerned and constantly turning to his rear end, the condition can be eased a little more quickly by getting a helper to hold the dog firmly, while you gently insert a child's-size glycerine suppository into the rectum. This will usually act quickly, and within a few minutes faeces will be passed.

INTERNAL PARASITES
Dogs may suffer from several types of worms, which include:
ROUNDWORM: The most common form is Toxocara Canis, which can be anything from about two inches to six inches in length. They look rather like pieces of string, but are pointed at both ends and cream or pale pink in colour. They are carried in the small intestine. If heavily infested, puppies may vomit worms of various sizes which are both immature worms and adult worms, or they may be passed through the anus. If adult dogs have roundworms, the worms may be passed in the faeces and are not actually seen.

Signs of worms in very young puppies include noisy breathing and nasal discharge, while puppies of the six to eight week age group may have diarrhoea or vomiting, a distended abdomen, and the coat will be tufty and not lie flat.

Any puppy with worms will not thrive as it should. All puppies should be wormed at least twice before going to new homes. Roundworms can be controlled by means of tablets or liquids. There are many on the market, or obtainable from your vet. Whatever you use, make sure you follow the instructions carefully.

TAPEWORM: These mostly affect adult dogs. They consist of a head which attaches to the wall of the small intestine, and from it grow white or greyish-white segments. These are shed at intervals, either in single segments or short chains of segments, and are passed along until expelled through the anus. At this point they may adhere to the hair around the anus, or to the outside of the faeces. They will look either like grains of rice, or flat like cucumber seeds. If heavily infested, the dog may be thin and out of condition. Control is effected by suitable worming preparations, but you must also make sure that the dog is free of fleas and lice, which act as intermediary hosts for tapeworm.

HOOKWORM: These are worms about three-eighths of an inch long, which live in the small intestine of the dog. They are most commonly found in working dogs such as pack hounds, but can be prevalent where dogs are exercised on grass. Hookworms can be controlled by regular dosing with a suitable worming preparation.

WHIPWORM: The name arises because the adult worms, which are found in the first part of the large intestine, look like a whip, and may be up to three inches in length. They can be prevalent in hot weather, especially where grass exercising runs are used. Not all infected dogs show any visible symptoms, but some may have diarrhoea. Whipworm is difficult to control and veterinary advice on worming is necessary.

HEARTWORM: This is a roundworm which affects the muscles of the heart. Fortunately, it is not found in Britain, but it is quite common in the USA, particularly in the warmer climates. It is also found in southern Europe and parts of Australia. The most likely way for the infection to be encountered in Britain is in an imported dog.

The clinical signs do not show for about six months after infection, but symptoms are unusual fatigue after exercise, coughing and loss of condition. Veterinary advice should be sought.

EXTERNAL PARASITES
These include fleas, lice, harvest mites, ticks, mange and ear mites.
FLEAS: These can cause irritation and the dog may nibble and chew the area of the flea bites, causing skin problems. Control is either by bathing with an insecticidal shampoo, or by the use of a suitable aerosol spray. As fleas do not actually breed on the dog, but in warm areas such as the dog's bedding, all bedding and places where the dog lies (e.g. by or near to a radiator) must also be treated with a spray.

LICE: There are two forms of lice which can affect the dog. One is a biting parasite, and the other a sucking parasite. Both can cause irritation, leading to itching and scratching. As lice are very slow-moving and live and breed on the dog, they are somewhat easier to deal with than fleas. There are many suitable shampoos on the market. If skin problems have arisen from heavy infestations, your vet will advise on suitable treatment.

HARVEST MITES (often referred to as Hay Mites): These cause severe irritation, and are picked up on the feet when dogs are exercised in country areas, usually in summer and autumn. They look like small orange or cream spots and cause irritation on the feet and lower part of the legs, and on the abdomen too in some dogs. Treatment consists of insecticidal shampoo.

TICKS: These are picked up when dogs are exercised and are more prevalent in some parts of the country than others. The commonest source of ticks is sheep. Ticks are greyish and bean-shaped in appearance, attach to the skin and draw blood from the dog, causing discomfort. Some pet shops now stock 'tick removers'. However, on the few occasions one of my dogs has had a tick, I have found the old trick of putting a spirit (surgical or methylated, or if these are not available, perfume will serve the same purpose) on to the tick where it is attached to the skin. This causes the tick to withdraw the head and suckers, and it can then be picked off. This should be done carefully, because if the head and suckers are not removed, it will leave a very sore and irritating spot which may become infected. My vet prefers to use a smear of Vaseline over the tick which causes it to die, when it can be removed.

MANGE
There are two classifications of Mange.
DEMODECTIC MANGE: This is caused by a parasite that lives in the hair follicle. Lesions may be localised or generalised. Localised Demodectic Mange is usually seen as small hairless patches on the head or forelimbs, and most typically as a spectacle effect of hair loss around the eyes. Generalised Demodectic Mange is a serious condition due to an immune deficiency and involves widespread hair loss, ridging of the skin, pustules due to secondary infection and considerable irritation and discomfort to the dog. There is often a distinctive 'mousey' smell.

SARCOPTIC MANGE: There has been a massive resurgence in Sarcoptic Mange in recent years due to contact with affected foxes, both urban and rural, and their environment. Typically, the appearance is of a scabby, moth-eaten, intensely irritating skin disorder. All cases of Mange require veterinary treatment.

EAR MITES: Tiny parasites living in the ear canal causing head shaking and a typical brown wax. Treatment consists of anti-parasitic ear drops. Your vet will advise.

INFECTIOUS DISEASES: Fortunately nowadays, due to successful vaccines, the outbreaks of the more common infectious diseases are kept down to a minimum. Infectious diseases are frequently transmitted by direct contact with an infected animal, but some, like Salmonella, are caused by contaminated food, so hygiene in food preparation areas is essential.

VACCINATION (OR INOCULATION): This is available against four main infectious diseases: Distemper; Leptospirosis; Parvovirus; and Infectious Hepatitis. The programme is quite simple, with two or more injections, two weeks apart. The duration of immunity created varies, and you should ask and follow your vet's advice. It is important that only healthy animals are vaccinated, as unhealthy ones may not have a good response to vaccination.

KENNEL COUGH: This is another infectious disease which is airborne, so one infected dog coughing or sneezing causes germs to spread to other dogs in the area. Good ventilation in a kennel will reduce the spread. Vets will advise on vaccination. It is important, in all cases where infectious or contagious diseases exist, to pay strict attention to hygiene, as it is of paramount importance.

COMMON SYMPTOMS

The following checklist was compiled by my vet, and represents some of the most common symptoms encountered by veterinary surgeons, and their possible causes. If any such symptoms appear in your dog, ask your vet for advice.

SYMPTOMS	POSSIBLE CAUSES
Closed eye	Corneal injuries; ulcer or foreign body.
Weepy or discharging eye	Conjunctivitis; tear duct problems.
Halitosis (bad breath)	Teeth or gum disorders; lip fold infection.
Head shaking, rubbing, or smelly ears	Ear infections; ear mites; foreign body or lice; skin disorders.
Excessive scratching, spots, redness. Weeping areas, hair loss	Skin problems; parasitic infections; allergies.
Lameness	Check for broken nails; foreign bodies in the foot; infections between pads.
Excessive thirst and urination	Diabetes; kidney failure; adrenal gland disorder; womb trouble.
Milk production	False pregnancy (may just be behavioural change).
Enlarged mammary glands	Mastitis, tumours.
Vulval discharge	Womb infection.
Exercise intolerance and coughing	Heart problems.
Abdominal enlargement	Pregnancy; dropsy due to heart failure; womb problems; liver disorders.
Increased frequency of urination	Cystitis; bladder stones; sequel to increased thirst.
Rubbing backside along the ground	Anal gland problems; perineal eczema; rarely, tapeworms.
Vomiting	Gastritis; gastro-enteritis or disease in other internal organ.

SYMPTOMS	POSSIBLE CAUSES
Acute diarrhoea	Usually casual infections or dietary changes. Withhold food and make electrolytes available.
Chronic diarrhoea	Either small bowel (malabsorption and weight loss) or large bowel (colitis, increased frequency, straining, mucus and blood).
Inability to climb stairs or jump	Back problems, usually painful and due to disc protrusion.

HEREDITARY PROBLEMS
Cockers have few problems believed to be of a hereditary nature, but they include:

FAMILIAL NEPHRITIS: This is a rare condition which affects the kidneys of young dogs, and proves fatal by eighteen to twenty four months of age. It affects the development of the kidneys which, on post-mortem examination, are seen to have a shrivelled appearance. Unfortunately there is no cure.

The Cocker Spaniel Club has investigated this, in co-operation with Cambridge University Veterinary College and the Animal Health Trust. A test is available on urine from any dog between nine and twenty-four months of age, which will show whether the dog has a predisposition to and is likely to develop Familial Nephritis or not. It will not show whether an animal carries the gene for it and, under certain circumstances, would transmit it to his progeny. Any vet can take a urine sample and send it to the Animal Health Trust for testing.

A geneticist who has studied the pedigrees of afflicted animals advises that the condition is inherited by means of a simple autosomal recessive gene. This means that both parents must carry the gene for the condition to be produced. The Cocker Spaniel Club has been monitoring the condition for about fifteen years, and has recorded about 100 cases during that period. The advice is that any dog or bitch having produced it should be withdrawn from breeding. Any reader with a Cocker which develops the condition, should send details to the Secretary of the Cocker Spaniel Club.

PROGRESSIVE RETINAL ATROPHY (PRA): This is a rare condition, occurring in only a very tiny minority of Cockers. It causes the blood vessels at the back of the eye to dry up. PRA can only be diagnosed with certainty by special ophthalmologist vets. The first indication that the condition exists may be some loss of vision in the half-light of evening, hence the original old-fashioned name of night blindness. The age of onset varies considerably, as does the age at which sight is badly affected and blindness may ensue. Unfortunately there is no cure.

There are a number of specialist ophthalmologists on a Kennel Club/British Veterinary Association panel who are able to test dogs for this condition, and who will issue certificates showing whether the dog is afflicted or clinically clear. Your vet will be able to refer you to one in your area.

It is believed that PRA is inherited by way of a simple autosomal recessive gene (i.e. both parents have to carry the gene for their progeny to have PRA). Specialist advice is that afflicted animals, their parents and their progeny should not be bred from. The Cocker Spaniel Club is monitoring the condition, and any cases should be notified to the honorary secretary.

OTHER PROBLEMS

UNCERTAIN TEMPERAMENT: On rare occasions a Cocker may have an uncertain temperament, whereby he will be loving and affectionate 99 per cent of the time, and for the other one per cent may show possessiveness or aggression. The eyes may become slightly glazed, the dog looks somewhat dazed, and yet after about twenty minutes or so is back to his normal affectionate self, not knowing what he has done.

In the UK the Cocker Spaniel Breed Council has been working for about twelve years, firstly with the Liverpool University Veterinary College and currently with Cambridge University Veterinary College, to try to establish what causes the condition. The Council feels that if only one Cocker is temperamental, it is one too many. Present research is investigating any link with epilepsy. A geneticist has found nothing to indicate that this is an hereditary problem.

Chapter Ten

THE COCKER SPANIEL WORLDWIDE

THE FCI COUNTRIES

In a great part of the world the recognised international authority for canine affairs is the Federation Cynologique Internationale, usually called the FCI. Its associated countries include countries in Europe and South America, most African countries, Australia and New Zealand. The FCI acknowledges the Breed Standard of the country of origin – in the case of Cockers that of the Kennel Club. The one main part of the world where this does not apply is the North American continent. There the Standard remains the property of the national breed clubs, although these are registered with, in the case of the US, the American Kennel Club.

Russian Ch. Wedelta's Goldigger: Top winning particoloured dog in 1993. Owned by Larissa Polegaiko.

I have judged in many countries in Europe, and in most of them the standard of the dogs is very high. I have been particularly impressed by the quality in Holland and Scandinavia, but everywhere there is keen competition at the top. In the last few years, exhibitors in Finland have been able to face different competition, because since the advent of rabies in Finland, dogs from Norway and Sweden (their old rivals) have not been allowed to travel there, and back into their own countries, without quarantine; so this has in effect killed off inter-Scandinavian travel between the three countries. Finnish exhibitors are now able to travel to mainland Europe, and sometimes face competition at home from European dogs.

Enthusiasm for the breed is also evident in the old Eastern bloc countries, and in Moscow and even as far away as Siberia I have found a determination to breed to improve the quality of their dogs. The national organisations are not yet ready to affiliate to the FCI, but the Cocker clubs are well organised and their shows are very successful. They are now able to collaborate with owners in neighbouring countries such as Finland and Sweden, with results that are becoming evident in the quality of the dogs. A couple of puppies have gone to Russia from Scotland – it will be interesting to see how they fare at Russian shows later.

THE AMERICAN SCENE
By Kate Romanski

In the last three decades the English Cocker Spaniel, though still fairly unknown to the American public, has become an extremely well-thought of competitor in American show rings. English Cockers of all colours have attained enviable show records, despite the fact that blue roans are still by far in the majority, and at times one has the feeling that a few American judges think the breed only comes in that distinctive color pattern.

THE AMERICAN KENNEL CLUB SYSTEM

The sport of dogs in America has grown tremendously since the end of World War II, as more and more dog lovers began to participate. Here in the USA, the primary governing body for both registrations and the various other aspects of the sport is the American Kennel Club (AKC), headquartered in New York City, with its registration facilities in Raleigh, North Carolina. The AKC also approves anyone wishing to judge, after a long period of provisional status. The current procedure and requirements can seem rather formidable to anyone aspiring to become a judge.

The main part of the dog sport is the conformation dog show, and when we refer to a Champion here, most of us are referring to an AKC 'Champion of Record', though there are other groups which offer titles. To complete a conformation championship, dogs are judged against the standard of perfection for the breed, as in other countries. An English Cocker Spaniel (or any breed recognized by the AKC) must earn fifteen points at a series of AKC licensed or member-club dog shows. No more than five points may be won at each event, and of course the ideal would be to accomplish this with your dog in three five-point shows! (In 1980 the black and white English Cocker bitch, Druid Little Miss

Muffet, owned by Marjorie Auster, won three five-point majors at a Friday/Saturday/Sunday series of shows in about 50 hours.)

The point ratings for each breed are calculated annually by the AKC, and depend on overall entries which vary from breed to breed and location to location. In order to win points, a dog must first win its class and then compete in the Winners Class with other first-place winners of its sex. The dog which takes Winners (Dog or Bitch) earns the points available that day, from one to five. The AKC also requires that dogs win at least two three-point shows or majors (i.e. a three-point, four-point or five-point win); so when you read that "so-and-so finished with three majors" this indicates the wins were in good competition.

Probably the main difference between American and British shows is that the AKC offers a Best of Breed Class in which finished (or 'made-up') Champions compete, along with the Winners Dog and Winners Bitch, and sometimes winners of non-regular classes such as Veteran, Field, and the like. The Best of Breed English Cocker then goes on to compete in the Sporting (Gundog) Group, and should it win this, will compete for Best in Show All-Breeds. When we have a show open only to one breed, it is termed a 'Specialty Show' and the winning dog is awarded Best of Breed – a great honor, especially if awarded by a breeder-judge.

English Cockers in America have won their share of all-breed Best in Shows, but none have accumulated the records of English Cockers in other countries. The American record-holder to date, with eighteen all-breed Best in Show wins, is Ch. Ancram's Simon (breeder/owner Joyce Scott Paine), a blue roan dog shown in the late 1960s and early 1970s.

For those wishing to introduce their English Cocker youngsters to dog shows, there are match shows sanctioned by the AKC, which are less formal, permitting entries at the gate on the day instead of weeks in advance. Match shows offer no points toward titles, but the overall format is similar to a regular show.

With about a dozen exceptions, all American shows are unbenched, which means you can come, show your dog, and leave. Well into the 1950s, most AKC shows were benched, but times change – though many long-time fanciers feel modern exhibitors do not have the chance to exchange ideas as happened when the benching rules required an all-day stay! The contemporary American dog show scene for English Cockers can be as large or as small as one desires (or one's budget permits). Some owners are content to strive for championships with their ECs as a goal in a breeding program. Others may not be interested, or may not be able to properly breed and raise young stock, so indulge themselves by going out for the various performance events in which ECs thrive, such as hunting tests, field trials, tracking, Obedience, and the newer Agility. Others enjoy the competition at the Best of Breed and Group level, and may 'campaign' their EC – a rather expensive proposition for an owner-handler. Still other owners employ the services of professional handlers, of whom we have a good number expert with the breed. For the most part, English Cockers enjoy 'showbiz' – we learn quickly about the ones who would prefer to be couch potatoes. In the competition of the 1990s, an unhappy, tail-down English Cocker could not make the cut!

Am. Ch. Jaybriars Heretic: BIS St. Charles, Missouri KC in May 1994, BIS at the National Specialty (ECSCA) 1994, and winner of many Sporting Groups in 1994. Owned by Judy Corbett.

Can. & Am. Ch. Wittersham's Charlemagne: No. I Eng. Cocker In USA All Systems, No. I in Canada twice. Bred and owned by Eugene Phoa.

Can. & Am. Ch. Wittersham's Debutante: Top winning bitch of the breed in Canadian history. Bred and owned by Eugene Phoa.

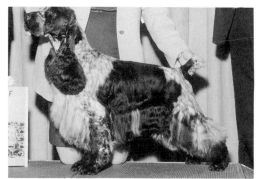

Am. Ch. Stage Doors Hoist The Flag: BoB American Spaniel Club, 1994. Bred by Randall K. Feather and Martin D. Sellers. Owned by Martin D. Sellers, Susan Ostermueller and Garret Feather.
Ashbey Photography.

Am. & Can. Ch. Ranzfel Ambassador: No. I English Cocker 1994, No. 10 Sporting Dog 1993.
Mikron Photos.

PROMINENT BREEDERS AND DOGS

Many individuals over the years have worked to bring the English Cocker Spaniel to its stature here today. As anyone who is familiar with the history of the breed in the USA is aware, the initial fanciers sought to preserve, protect and improve the Cocker Spaniel of England when America's 'Cocker Spaniel' was evolving in a different direction, which eventually gave the world the glamorous American Cocker of today. The English Cocker was fortunate to be blessed with a number of intelligent, clever and caring individuals in the years after World War II who worked with their American-bred stock, and, from time to time, brought in some of the best Cockers Britain had to offer. Sometimes this worked; sometimes it didn't, but the breeders persevered.

The dog which made the modern English Cocker here, whelped in 1964 of a pedigree blending older American and more recent British lines, was the blue roan dog, Ch. Dunelm Galaxy, bred by Dr and Mrs Arthur Ferguson. The sire of 93 AKC Champions when he died in 1977, Galaxy is behind almost every parti-color line as well as a few solid lines of our contemporary English Cockers. His get and grand-get made even greater records number-wise, but Galaxy still deserves the credit when you look at the overall picture of American-bred English Cockers in the past 25 years. A Galaxy grandson, the blue roan dog Ch. Kenobo Capricorn (Helga Tustin/Bonnie Threlfall), is the all-time top producer with 121 champion get.

Next in line after Galaxy himself is Ch. Olde Spice Crusader (Vicky Spice) with 65 Champion get to date. His background is a blend of several American lines interestingly combined with British imports. Like his forebears Galaxy and Capricorn, Crusader, also a blue roan, has set his stamp on the modern American-bred EC, producing many winners and top producers. His daughter, Ch. Olde Spice Sailors Beware, blue roan, bred and owned by Vicky Spice, holds the distinction of winning Best of Breed at the ECSCA National Specialty three times (1985, 1986 and 1989), a record not challenged to date. (And if you study the pedigree of the 1994 winner, Ch. Jaybriar's Heretic, also a blue roan bitch, you will find that three-quarters of her background tracks to Galaxy, with the rest made up of Reklawholms (Prudence Walker), Sohos (Lynn Clark) and Birchwyns (Mary Livesey Parish MD).The solid-color English Cocker in the USA will never claim the producing records of our parti-colors, simply because there are fewer of them. However, in recent years, solid reds have been our top winners in the show ring, British imports and American-bred alike. The overall quality of the solid colors, in decline for many, many years, has now made a turnaround and they are winning their share of honors, proving to the doubters that a good English Cocker is a good English Cocker, regardless of color!

It is to be regretted, in a way, that the strict British quarantine laws preclude most exchanges of stock between the USA and Britain, as possibly the USA could give back to your shores a part of what we have had from the UK over the years to help make the breed here so attractive and delightful.

AUSTRALIA

By BARBARA KILLWORTH (CABAL)

The Australian Show scene consists mostly of Championship Shows where points

towards the title of Australian Champion can only be obtained in the following manner:
Minor Puppy: Six-nine months of age
Puppy: Six-twelve months of age
Junior: Six-eighteen months of age
Intermediate: 24-36 months of age
Australian-Bred or State-Bred: Open to all dogs over the age of six months born in Australia, or in some States, born in that State.
Open: Open to all dogs over the age of six months.

All first placings in the respective classes return to the ring to compete for the Challenge award. Six points are given to the Best Dog and Best Bitch chosen for the Challenge, plus one point for each dog beaten with a maximum of 25 points being awarded at the one show. The dogs need to gain 100 Challenge points, with no more than two Challenges being won under the same judge, to gain their Australian title.

At most Cocker Spaniel Breed Speciality shows the solids and parti-colours are judged separately but all compete in the final challenge line-up for the Challenge award.

JUDGING ORGANISATION

In Australia we do not have as many Speciality shows, as our judging panel consists of many more all-rounders than specialists. Most of our current judges are the product of our recent Judges Training Scheme, rather than coming through the ranks of breeders, which is more the case in England. With many more Championship Shows being held than in England, it is much easier to gain your title here. Several Championship Shows are even held on the same day. The majority of shows are held out of doors, as opposed to the English benched shows. Each State has its own Governing Body with the most prestigious show in the calendar year being their own Royal Agricultural Show – the Royal Challenge being a most sought-after award by all breeders, with the top breeders travelling throughout the Australian States each year to compete at these different 'Royals'. Our judges have to pass a fairly stringent written examination, and a fairly contrived practical because we do not have training shows for them to gain this experience. Their final examinations are done by a panel of licensed judges. After passing their first group, candidates usually progress through the other six groups to reach all-breed status. If successful, a judge can reach this level in a period of seven years.

Because our dogs are exhibited at the major fixtures under many overseas judges, mainly from America, Europe and England, we have to present our dogs in three different options of presentation. We therefore display a middle-of-the-road attitude to presentation, probably a little too much coat for the English, and not enough for the Americans.

TOP WINNING DOGS

To mention just a few dominant dogs that have made their mark among the Cockers now being exhibited is not an easy task. The dogs mentioned below have not only done this, but all in their own right have been top winners in the show ring as well.

Aust. Ch. Marsden Time Traveller (Ch. Marsden Time Flies – Ch. Fairanchor April Star): This dog has had a significant influence on the breed in Australia.

Aust. Ch. Cabal The Luv Machine (Ch. Marsden Blue Venture – Ch. Creole Cat Balou): A prolific winner in the show ring with many winning offspring. Photo: Michael M. Traford.

Ch. Dandaul Dubarry
Sire: Dongelly High Venture (imp. in dam) by High Venture of Ware ex Ewhurst Pentavy Pompadour.
Dam: Dandaul Yum Yum by Colinwood Pawnee ex Edenbar Cindy Lou.

Ch. Brightleaf Bewinged
Sire: Ch. Feenix Fly By Night   **Dam:** Brightleaf Be Gracious
'Wings' was a double-up on Winter Yana of Weirdene. He was a dog that must be regarded as the most influential sire of his day. He produced many, many champions, a number of which, like their father, also went on to be top producers. 'Wings', with the combination of the Dubarry lines, has been the basis of most of the top winning parti-colour kennels in the Eastern States of Australia. Not only was he a producer, he himself won many Cocker Speciality shows, Royals and All-Breed shows, under Breed Specialists and All-Breed judges alike.

Ch. Cabal The Luv Machine
Sire: Ch. Marsden Blue Venture   **Dam:** Ch. Creole Cat Balou (a 'Wings' daughter)

Ch. Brightleaf Bewinged (Ch. Feenix Fly By Night – Ch. Brightleaf Be Gracious): The most influential sire of his day.   Photo: Michael M. Traford.

Ch. Glenayden Snow Storm: Best in Show at the first Australian National, under Richmond Weir.

Once again a very dominant sire and show winner for his owners Sid and Edna Flynn, producing many winners including the Best in Show Sydney Royal winner, Ch. Lehearn Lovem 'n' Leave Em, whose offspring also left a trail of winners behind them. His wins included many All-Breed BIS, Speciality and Royal wins, including BIS at Sydney Royal, 1982.

Ch. Marsden Time Traveller
Sire: Ch. Marsden Time Flies   **Dam:** Fairanchor April Star
He too is another of the top producing lines. This dog is now thirteen years of age, and is still a strong influence on the breed and producing champions. He is a grandson of 'Wings', and has won multiple BIS at Speciality Shows, Royals and All-Breed shows.

These have been my impressions of dogs that I have personally seen or owned in NSW, and not interstate. Although some of the present Cockers are winning well, there are no dominant dogs that stand out both in show and in get. Current winners include: Frank Werner's Ch. Glenbriar Blue Grass, who has won, but not yet produced a Champion; Julie Gotch's black bitch Ch. Clarevale Lochdene Mirth, who has done most of the winning in solids, but has not yet been bred from; and my own and Grahme Wright's Aust. and NZ Ch. Classicway Certain Style (imp. UK), with two of her children by Eng. Sh. Ch. Classicway Country Life of Kendalwood who have achieved their titles.

AUTHOR'S NOTE
Barbara Killworth was very modest when writing this article for me, as she omitted to say that she was joint owner, with Mrs Mac Formston (Brightleaf), of Ch. Brightleaf Bewinged. In fact, Barbara handled and campaigned 'Wings' in the show ring.
    I never saw 'Wings', but I did judge Ch. Marsden Time Traveller (then a Veteran) a few

years ago and made him Res. Best Dog at the Cocker National in Adelaide He was a lovely type dog and a very good showman, capably handled by his co-owner/breeder, Frank Werner.

I found it very interesting to read an article on Cocker Spaniels from the Sporting Spaniel Newsletter, on the same lines as our own Kennel Club Judges Choice article, in which top breeders are asked for their opinion on the greatest specimens of the breed. In the Australian article, several judges, when asked for their choice of the three greatest specimens, named Ch. Brightleaf Bewinged and Ch. Cabal the Luv Machine. Ch. Marsden Time Traveller was also in the reckoning. All seemed to agree that, not only were these dogs exceptionally good in the show ring, they were exceptionally good producers too, and of great benefit to the breed.

Barbara also failed to say that Ch. Cabal Stare 'n' Whisper (by Ch. Marsden Time Flies ex Ch. Creole Cat Balou [dam of Cabal The Luv Machine]) holds the Australian record for Royal Challenges, having won seven.

SOUTH AFRICA FROM 1980 TO 1995
By FRAN MINAAR

For many years Cocker Spaniels have been popular house pets, and were among the more popular breeds as show dogs. Times have changed, and today both parents in a family often have full-time jobs, and the younger members become involved in other outdoor activities. As a result, short-coated dogs have taken over in popularity because less grooming and show preparation are necessary.

KUSA AND BREED CLUBS
All dog Clubs are affiliated to the Kennel Union of South Africa and hold both Non Championship or Open Shows as well as Championship Shows, governed by KUSA rules. South Africa is divided into several geographical centres according to the registration numbers. These centres incorporate all the big cities where several All Breed Clubs exist. The respective committees organise activities such as training classes and lectures, as well as one or two Non Championship Shows and one Championship Show per annum.

In the 1960s there was an upsurge in interest in showing Cocker Spaniels and others, and Breed and Group Clubs were formed. To date there are still only two Cocker Spaniel Clubs. The Western Province Cocker Spaniel Club held its first Championship Show in 1966, and holds one Open Show per annum plus other activities, lectures and grooming classes. This Club is based in Cape Town. The Transvaal Cocker Spaniel Club is based in Johannesburg, and has been in existence since 1962, covering the same activities. Their first Championship Show was held in 1987.

Both these Clubs hold Open Shows once or twice per year, with one of these being a Trophy Show, sometimes held in conjunction with All Breed Championship Shows. Hence, there was always an incentive for keener exhibitors to travel to different centres for their Shows, as Challenge Certificates are on offer at the All Breed Championship

Shows. In those early days, 30-40 Cockers would be entered at the All Breed Ch. Shows.

The Breed Clubs had to qualify to hold a Championship Show. The present qualification is an entry of at least 30-35 exhibits, present on the day of the Show. These numbers must be maintained or Championship Status is withdrawn until further Qualifying Shows meet the requirements. The Transvaal Cocker Spaniel Club usually has about 50-60 exhibits at a Championship Show, and Western Province just manages the required number, as there are fewer breeders and regular exhibitors in the Cape Town area.

For a dog or bitch to become a Show Champion they must win five points in all, but in the minimum of two centres. A CC can be worth one or two points according to the number of exhibits present in each sex (if less than ten in one sex, only one point; if more than ten present, two points).

Dogs and bitches which have already attained their Champion Status may still compete for further CCs or enter only in a Champions Class, which is a restricted class. They are thus not eligible for a CC, but they do compete against the CC winners for Best of Breed. The dog or bitch must be over nine months of age for a CC to count towards their Champion status, and at least one CC must be awarded at over eighteen months of age. All Championship Shows must offer classes for Minor Puppy (six-nine months), Puppy (nine-twelve months), Junior, Graduate and Open. Further classes are optional in the breed section as are Challenge Classes and Stakes, e.g. Best Puppy in Show, and so on.

The Specialist or Breed Clubs work on the same system but have more 'Special Classes' to add interest to the proceedings, and to encourage novice exhibitors to come back. Travel is expensive, as Cape Town to Durban, or Johannesburg to Cape Town, involves a journey of about 1,000 miles (1,600 kms). This could mean an overnight stop en route if travelling by car. Then at least two nights' accommodation in the Show-holding centre. The more affluent owners travel by air and hire transport at the other end. Everyone owns travelling boxes or wire cages as Shows are no longer benched and are all held outdoors, regardless of the weather. To make such journeys worthwhile the Cocker Clubs usually hold their Championship Shows over a weekend that coincides with other Championship Shows. One can sometimes compete for three sets of CCs over one weekend.

At All Breed Championship Shows CCs are offered regardless of the numbers entered in a breed. There may only be one Cocker dog or bitch entered, but if the judge considers it worthy it will be awarded a one point CC. So it is up to the judges to maintain a high standard. It would appear to be quite easy to make up a dog under our present system. As a result, a more prestigious award is a Best in Show, won at a Cocker Club Show, or a Gundog Group winner. Even better is Best in Show at an All Breed Championship Show. In this day and age of imported Champions in various breeds, such an award is highly prized. Not many of our Cockers have managed to achieve this honour in recent shows.

Cocker Spaniels still remain popular house pets but numbers have dropped on the Show scene – sometimes only ten or twelve in all at an All Breed Championship Show, and one or two at an Open Show. The general public still have the golden Cocker as their first preference. Many have had disappointments because of uncertain temperaments, and the entire breed is labelled accordingly. It must be stressed that these problems have come mainly from 'backyard' breeders – very often unregistered and from unknown backgrounds. Dog Clubs do try to educate the public on such issues. First-time Cocker owners are encouraged to join a Club, and thus learn more about their dogs. Many Cocker owners purchase a good dog or bitch, have an odd litter, exhibit at a few shows and then cannot be bothered because of the trimming required, so attend for the social side. As a result show-quality litters are not so plentiful, and interested puppy buyers are not prepared to wait for expected litters.

IMPORTANT LINES
Cocker imports that have dominated our quality stock have all come from the UK. Kennel names that appear most frequently in our breeding stock are:
Solids: Kavora, Sorbrook, Helenwood, Canyonn, Styvechale and very recently Charbonnel, Crankwoods, and Lochdene. Particular solid imports that have graced the show ring with success have been:
SA Ch. Sorbrook Mulberry at Braganza (black)
SA Ch. Sorbrook Dilly Dally at Barradell (golden)
SA Ch. Sorbrook Stormy Night (black)
SA Ch. Kavora Cointreau at Nawhaven (black)
SA Ch. Kavora Carbon Copy at Barradell (black)
SA Ch. Styvechale Satin Slippers (golden)
SA Ch. Helenwood Harvest Moon (golden)
SA Ch. Canyonn Silhouette (black)
Progeny from some of the above have also made their mark.

Particolour imports who have made their mark have come from Craigleith, Bitcon, Randline, Coltrim, Yardew, Kendalwood and Lynwater. Of particular note are:
SA and Eng. Sh. Ch. Craigleith Sweet Charity
SA Ch. Craigleith The Arcadian of Chance (orange and white)
SA Ch. Craigleith Lord of the Rings (blue roan)
SA Ch. Craigleith Waltztime (tricolour)
SA Ch. Craigleith Song and Dance of Chance (blue roan)
SA Ch. Randline Deep Reflection of Ide (blue roan)
SA Ch. Bitcon Midnight Ranger (blue roan)
SA Ch. Bitcon Rock-a-Billy (blue roan)
SA Ch. Bitcon Broken Dreams (blue roan)
SA Ch. Coltrim Blue Print (blue roan)
SA Ch. Coltrim Snowbird (black and white)
SA Ch. Kendalwood Designer Model of Ole (blue roan)
Here again, progeny from these imports represent the breeding and show stock that are currently about.

All Breed Competitions do exist throughout the South African dog world and KUSA now runs an All Breed Championship Show every two years, where Special Classes are offered. Time and money are necessary to campaign a good Cocker, so we probably have many good specimens that go unsung. Dog showing is quite a popular hobby in SA, but predominantly within the European community. With the advent of the 'New South Africa' and more education about and exposure to the keeping of pedigree dogs, the interest is spreading to other sections of the community.

Tail docking in Cockers is a talking point, and is now optional for breeders. We use the British Standard, but undocked specimens will not be penalised in the show ring. Should the ban ever be seriously adhered to in the UK and on the Continent, there is a murmur that breeders may consider looking elsewhere for future imports.

REQUIREMENTS FOR JUDGES

Qualifications for judges on the Local scene have been updated in recent years. It is necessary for aspiring judges to apply to KUSA to judge either a single breed or group at one time. Experience in any of the recognised canine activities, e.g. breeding, showing, or stewarding, is necessary before being accepted.

Examination:

1a.) KUSA Constitution and Rules applicable to Shows.

1b.) Anatomy, skeletal structure and movement of the dog, with terms used.

1c.) 80 per cent pass mark required.

When these requirements have been met, the candidate must then judge at a minimum of two Non Championship Shows and write reports on first and second placings in each class judged. Reports must cover at least eight exhibits in the required breed or breeds within that group, usually requiring appointments at more than two shows. When sufficient reports have been approved by KUSA, candidates move on to the next written examination which covers the Breed Standards in that Group as well as judging etiquette and ring procedure. When an 80 per cent pass mark has been achieved, aspirant judges are then placed on a list of judges eligible to judge that Breed or Group at Championship Show level. To qualify as a judge at Best in Show All Breeds at Championship Show level, the judge must be on the KUSA Panel for at least four Groups.

Judges from countries other than the UK should be on the approved list of their own country. UK Judges should have awarded CCs in the UK in the breeds to be judged, or have written proof of sufficient experience of breeds judged at Non Championship Show level in the UK. All are subject to KUSA approval. Because of the expense involved in importing judges from other countries, it is always an advantage for judges to have the required experience in judging more than one breed or Group. Clubs can then share expenses for a judge who can then alternate Groups at different Shows held over one weekend. Cocker folk who have judged out here recently include Joan Iredale, Moray Armstrong, John Gillespie, Ed and Joan Simpson, and Kay Holmes.

GERMANY
By HERBERT KLEMANN, Chairman, Spaniel Club Deutschland

The Cocker Spaniel in Germany is very much influenced by imports from Britain. Cockers important for the breeding system either are imports (males or females) or imports will be found in the first, or at least second, generation of their pedigree. In general, the population of Cockers is divided into 60 per cent particolours and 40 per cent solids. At shows here, the colours are separated into particolours, reds, blacks and 'other solids', which includes chocolate, black and tans, sables, etc.

MAKING UP CHAMPIONS

We have two kinds of German Champion awards. One is given by the German Kennel Club (VDH) and one by the Breed Club. For the German Champion (Kennel Club) the dog has to win the class (Open, Working, or Champion class) four times – twice at All Breed Shows and twice at Specialties – and one year and one day has to elapse between the first and the last win. Considering that the colours are separated, it is not too difficult for a dog to win this title, but perhaps for particolours it is more difficult, due to higher numbers of entries at shows.

The German Champion (Club) is more difficult. There are four Spaniel Clubs in Germany, The 'Spaniel Club Germany' has the following system. The class winners of the Open, Working, and Champion Class of all colours have to compete, and only the winner will get the CAC. Four CACs – notwithstanding whether from specialties or All Breed Shows – are required under three different judges in two different parts of Germany. Also one year and one day has to elapse between the first and the last win.

Another title is the International Champion, 'Champion Internationale de Beaute' (Ch.I.B.). A dog has to win four CACIBs, only given at All Breed Shows, and granted, like the Club CAC, in three different countries (one country has to be the home country of the dog) under three different judges with the same time gap. In addition, working dogs like Cockers, have to pass a field trial.For permission to breed, every dog has to have the hips examined, and a German judge, a requirement by the German Kennel Club (VDH), has to confirm that the dog is constructed according to the standard.

The Spaniel Club Germany aims to assign as many English judges as possible, because it is very important and interesting for every Cocker Spaniel breeder to have the opinion of a judge from the breed's country of origin.

AUSTRIA
By Maria-Luise Doppelreiter (Osterreichring).
IMPORTANT BREEDERS AND DOGS

In Austria, Rosemary Charrington (Hilltop) has been the most influential breeder in the last 35 years. Her dogs are based on the best English lines (Scolys, Haradwaithe, Ouaine, Merrybray, Weirdene, Blenkarn, of Ware, Cilleine, to name just a few) and she was always very successful in mixing her lines with good English imports. Most of the 'young' Austrian breeders, who are successful in the show ring now, have based their lines on Hilltop breeding. Very influential sires were the imported Merrybray Monarua (by Matagowrie of Merrybray), Sandstorm of Hilltop (by Monarua out of Shady Lady of Hilltop, a very successful daughter of Scolys Stablemate, a Starduster son from France), Globe Trotter of Hilltop (by Cilleine Echelon) and his son, my Hi! Jack of Hilltop (out of Corn Dolly of Hilltop, a grand-daughter of Sandstorm), and his half-brother Lollipop of

German Ch. Estee Lauder Vom Osterreichring (Bullpark Blue Lightning – Up-To-Date Of Black Castle). Bred and owned by Maria-Luise Doppelreiter.

Austrian Ch. Emma Peel Vom Osterreichring: Sister to Ch. Estee Lauder, and a top winner in the show ring. Owned by V.G. Raithofor

Raitis Diana V.D. Hohen Veitsch: A daughter of Ch. Emma Peel.

Hilltop (out of the Sandstorm daughter Lemon Tree of Hilltop), Dearnewood Stars and Stripes (by Mistfall Meddler), Earl Grey v. Osterreichring (by Bullpark Blue Lightning out of a Hi! Jack daughter) and Dirty Dancer v. Osterreichring (by Hi! Jack) in particolours. In solids, the lines are wider spread, mostly based on hunting lines (going back to Eldwythe Eastwind). A very much used Austrian-bred stud dog was Hatstone's Black Diamond (by Niggel Caterra), but most of the stud dogs used in solids are German-bred (Aro's, Caterra, Heidebusch), English (Lochranza) or Dutch breeding (Korden's, Bitchen, Tripol's).

LITTERS AND PUPPIES
For a small country we have quite a few litters. In 1993 there were 28 Cocker litters (eighteen particolour, ten solid) with 136 puppies and eleven imports (from Germany, Netherlands, Hungary, Czechoslovakia, Slovenia and Croatia). This year will bring us increasing numbers after a period of stagnation some years ago. To be bred from, a Cocker must have at least the grading of 'very good' at two shows and a good hip-score. If stud dogs from other countries are used they must be admitted for breeding in their home country. All puppies of a litter must be registered at the age of three weeks, and they all get official OKV (Austrian Kennel Club) pedigrees when sold. Every mating must be reported to the 'breeding warden' within ten days at most.

AUSTRIAN SHOW SCENE
In Austria we have six International All Breed Shows and five National All Breed Shows, as well as one National Club-Winnershow. CACIB is only awarded at International Shows, while the Austrian CACA can be won at these and at the National Shows. In addition we have one or two Club shows every year, at which only the Club CCs are awarded, no CACA or CACIB. To become an Austrian Champion a dog must win four CACAs, three of which must be won in the Field Trial Class. For the International Champion title, a dog must win two CACIBs and be placed at an international Field Trial with not less than 70 per cent of the winner's points. The title of Club-Champion can be won without a Field Trial, but one of the four tickets has to be won from the annual Club-Winners show. All colours compete together. CACIB and CACA are not awarded in the Junior classes, but the dogs can win best Junior, and three such wins make them up into an Austrian Jugendshampion. (Junior Champion).

We have Puppy Class (six-nine months), Junior (nine-eighteen months), Open (over fifteen months), Champion, Field Trial and Not for Competition. Every dog gets a grading (excellent, very good, good, sufficient, insufficient), and the best four of the excellent and very good graded dogs are placed from first to fourth in each class. The 1st excellent winners of Open, Champion and Field Trial class can win a CACA and compete for the CACIB. The 2nd excellent in each of these classes can get the Res. CACA, and the dog who was beaten only by the CACIB winner competes for the Res. CACIB. The tickets are given in both sexes. Competitors for the Best of Breed are the two best Juniors and the two CACIB winners. The number of Club CCs given depends on the number of entries per breed.

All BOB winners can compete in the Group. There is a different group system under the FCI from that in Britain. Spaniels compete in Group 8, which includes the hunting (Spaniels and German Wachtelhund), retrieving (all Retrievers) and water dogs (Portuguese water dogs, Koikerhondje).

Our club is represented with special shows at all Austrian shows, which means that we can select the judges ourselves. We do have quite a number of foreign judges. Recently we have had judges from Germany, Hungary, Slovenia, Czechoslovakia, Sweden, Italy, France and Britain. The difficulty about inviting English judges is that most of them are specialised in one or two of the Spaniel breeds, and as our club looks after all Spaniel breeds, we can only invite those who are allowed to judge them all at CC level.

At our bigger shows we have between 1,000 and 3,000 dogs of all breeds and competition in Cockers is usually quite good, with entries of about 40 to 100. At our annual Club Winners show we have very good entries, and in 1994 we had 154 Spaniels from all eight breeds. At these shows we also have some additional classes: Veteran (which will also be at the other shows from 1995); Baby class (up to six months); Bred by exhibitor; and Class of honour. This makes it easier for exhibitors to show more dogs, and so the number of entries is increasing every year.

EDUCATION OF JUDGES
In Austria a judge must first be ring secretary on three occasions, then he has to be an assistant judge at three shows. Cynological knowledge is taught in a seminar (three days), which includes anatomy, judging, writing reports, knowledge on all breeds, standards, genetics and organisation of the OKV, and FCI. Next comes a theoretical exam and after passing this a potential judge must judge six dogs per breed (in very rare breeds he can be examined theoretically). The judges have to judge for at least two years in Austria before they can judge outside the country. The new FCI rules do not allow judges to handle other people's dogs; they are only allowed to handle dogs in their ownership or bred by them.

HOLLAND
By Haja Van Wessem (Spegglewaggel)

There are between fifteen and twenty All Breed Championship Shows per year and one Championship Show of the Spaniel Club. In Belgium there are about ten All Breed shows and one Club Show. In Germany there are about ten All Breed Championship Shows and about twenty Championship Shows of the Clubs (Jagdspaniel Klub and Spaniel Club Deutschland).

The Open Show as held in England is hardly known on the Continent. There are two kinds of shows – CAC shows and CACIB shows. At a CAC show, the CC for the Dutch title is given to the best dog and best bitch, provided they were graded Excellent, no matter which class they were in. At a CACIB show, the CAC is offered and also the CACIB for the title of International Champion, but it need not be awarded to the same dog. The CAC may be won from any class, but the CACIB may only be awarded to the winner of Open, Field Trial or Champion classes.

To become a Dutch or German Champion, the dog must have won four CACs under three different judges. In Holland the last one must be won after the dog has reached the age of 27 months. In Germany there must be 12 months between the first and last CAC. To become an International Champion the dog must have won two CACIBs under two

Dutch Ch. Tripol's Julio (Canyonn Collaborator – Tripol's I'm Classy): Best in Show at the Cocker Club of Holland Ch. Show 1994. Bred and owned by Mrs A. Bodgers-Dam.

Dutch Ch. Snugglewood's Andante (Tripol's Acition – Tripol's Judy Boopy): Cocker of the Year in Holland 1991, 1992 and 1993. Bred and owned By C.A.F. Warmenhoven.

different judges in two different countries (one of which must be the country of origin of the breed or the home-country of the owner) and a first, second or third prize in a Field Trial. Between the first and the last CACIB there must be a period of twelve months.

In Holland, the minimum age for showing is nine months, and Classes scheduled are:
Junior: Nine to eighteen months.
Open: Fifteen months and over.
Champion: For dogs with the title of Champion in any country.
Field Trial: For dogs having won a prize at a National or International Field Trial.
Breeders' class (owner/breeder) may also be scheduled, but is not compulsory.

IMPORTANT DOGS

The first Cocker to be registered in the Dutch Stud Book (1890) was 'Wallace', a liver and white. Influential breeders include:-

Dr and Mrs F. van Herwaarden, whose kennel name was Wagtail, were influential from 1924 until about 1965. The foundation dog 'Fatty' came from Belgium, and the bitch Brockland Fan and the dog Duke of Chelmsford came from England.

Mrs H. A. van Rees-Schirmbeck (Marewende) was influential from around 1935 to 1960 with, among others, the imports Syne of Ware, Miss Cinders of Ware, Brilliant Queen of Ware, Fairwings of Ware and Southfield Saucy Sally of Ware.

Dr and Mrs C. Langhout (Urtica) who have featured since before the war until now, with imports such as Colinwood Cossack (brother to Ch. Colinwood Cowboy); their most famous top-winning dog was Ch. Urtica's Noble, who later went to the Scholerberg kennel of Mrs Schulz in Germany. Mrs Schulz had imported from England Courtdale Sub Lieutenant, a son of Flag Lieutenant. He was used extensively and sired lovely typey puppies. His influence was important.

Mr G. Herzog from Germany imported Matagowrie of Merrybray who, among others, sired Ch. Tripols Funny Faisal, sire of Ch. Tripol's Dreamlight. Both were of great influence on Dutch particolour Cockers.

In recent years imports who became Champions and/or who produced Champions were: Cochise Conundrum (1980s), Kavora Summer Wine, Kavora Campari Boy, Hazari High Hope, Atkia Eldorado, Avandora First Selection at Mondanou, Lindridge Salute and Bobbinbrae's Solitaire of Cornbow.

Two of the top-winning dogs are: Birchen Beau Brummel, Dutch Ch., World Champion in 1990 and 1991, German, Lux. Ch., Cocker of the Year 1989 and 1990 (Hemany's Tobias x Soother's Briquet), breeder/owner Aldert Kuiper; and Dutch Ch. Snugglewood's Andante, Junior World Champion 1991, German and Lux. Ch. (Ch. Tripol's Acition x Ch. Tripol's Judy Boopy), bred and owned by C. Warmenhoven, Cocker of the Year 1991, 1992 and 1993.

HUNGARY
By Thomas Jakkel, President, Spaniel Club of the Hungarian Kennel Club (MEOE)

In Hungary, there are two Spaniel Clubs:

1.) Spaniel Club of the Hungarian Kennel Club (MEOE), established in 1967, with 1,400 members, of which I have the honour to be President.

2.) Hungarian Spaniel Club, established in 1989 with 450 members.

The Cocker Spaniel is the second most popular breed in Hungary (the first being the German Shepherd). There are eleven or twelve National All Breed Shows (CAC) every year, and five or six International (CACIB) shows. The biggest Spaniel Show is the Club Championship Show every year. There are 50-80 entries at the Nationals, 100-150 at the Internationals, and between 180 and 210 entries at the Club Show.

The only Hungarian-bred World Champion Cocker is Int. Ch. Highland Pride of Black Mirage (which I bred and owned), who won her Junior World Champion title in 1992 in

Int. Ch. Northworth Product Of Play (Int. Ch. Tanac's Play It Again – Int. Eur. & Finnish Ch. Northworth Vulgar Taste): Cocker Of The Year, Hungary 1993, Jun. Euro Ch. 1992. Bred by Nina Kauhanen (Finland), owned by Dr T. Jakkel.

Int. & Hung. Ch. Lochranza Black Mirage (Sh. Ch. Canyon Carbon Copy – Lochranza Carol Ann): Cocker of the Year 1994, Hungary. VDH Euro Ch. 1994, winner in five different countries. Bred by Miss Macmillan & Mrs J. Gillespie, owned by Dr T. Jakkel.

Spain under John Gillespie (GB). My Club has some very good international contacts, because I have judged in sixteen different countries in the last five years. We have enjoyed the judging of several English judges in Hungary, including Ed Simpson, Leslie Page, Penny Lester, Peter Rudd, Moray Armstrong, Peter Morgan, Ken Rees and Robin Sadler.

French Ch. Fiston Malin Du Talai: 1992 and 1993 Group & Multiple CACIB Winner, BIS Spaniel Club Francais and the Paris Ch. Show, Top Cocker in France 1992 and 1993. Owned by Mme Fabrice Brisset.

Port. Ch. & World Ch. 1994 Chataway Craftsman (Sorbrook Countryman – Fireline Red Amber). Bred by David Todd (UK), owned by Carlos Farinha Dos Santos

Pictured left to right: Sp. Ch. Yearling Most Welcome, Sp. Ch. Yearling Inch By Inch, and Yearling Only In Autumn. Owned by Marisa de Elorza.

SCANDINAVIA
By ANJA PUUMALA (Leavenworth)

Looking at old lists of Cockers of the Year, it is easy to see that in Scandinavia two combinations appear to dominate as show and stud dogs in each country.

In particolours, it was Ch. Celeste of Helenwood mated to Ch. Deewell Senator. From this mating came such big winners as Ch. Travis Jive Talkin, Ch. Travis Mary's Pledge, Ch. Travis Tribute to Helenwood, Ch. Travis Spot On, Ch. Travis Celestes Flair and Ch. Travis Tweed Effect. In solids, an influential mating was Int. Ch. Leavenworth Butter Kiss (by Ch. Lochranza Farmer's Boy out of a daughter of Astrawin Apollo) mated to Ch. Bidston Solomon. From that mating I got Ch. Leavenworth Kissing Success (Cocker of the Year in Sweden for three years), Int. Ch. Leavenworth Secret Kisses, Ch. Leavenworth Tradition, Int. Ch. Leavenworth Kisses for Sale, Int. Ch. Leavenworth Trick of Kisses, Ch. Leavenworth Kiss of Fire and Ch. Leavenworth Kissing Thing.

Ch. Bidston Solomon (bred by Vera Hillary in England) has certainly been the stud dog who has meant most in solid breeding in Scandinavia in the 1980s. His daughter, Int. Ch. Leavenworth Secret Kisses mated to Ch. Leavenworth Lucky Strike (son of Ch. Astrawin Apollo) produced Ch. Leavenworth It's a Pleasure, who is behind almost every winner in Sweden and Norway. Even in Finland we have many of his grandchildren.

NORWAY

The winning kennels in Norway are Ar-Ha-Bo in particolours with their Classicway lines, the owner being Heyerdahl Larsen. In the 1980s Dag Linna won a lot with his Tanac's solid Cockers. He started with Travis bloodlines, but does not breed any more.

Ann Lund started with Travis and Astrawin dogs and used Astrawin Apollo and Leavenworth Lucky Strike. Her prefix is Timankas and her dogs are winning well at the

*Int. Norw. & Finnish Ch. Carillo Call
For Pleasure: Cocker of the Year in
Norway 1987, 1988, 1989 And 1991.
Owned by Kari Granaas Hansen.*

*Norw. & Swed. Ch. Carillo Chubby
Checker: Cocker of the Year Norway
1990, 1992 and 1993, Spaniel of the
Year and No. 4 Top Winning Dog All
Breeds 1993. Owned by Kari Granaas
Hansen.*

*Swed. Ch. Charbonnel A One's Macho:
BIS Swed. Cocker Club Ch. Show, 1993,
and Best Male and Reserve BIS Swed.
Cocker Club Ch. Show 1994. Bred By
Sandy Platt, owned by Ann Olsson.*

*Norw. Ch. Bomway Safe Landing.
Owned by Brit and Jostein Halvorsen.*

present time. Kari Granaas-Hansen (Carrillo Cockers) is breeding both solids and particolours. Her big winner is a red bitch, daughter of Leavenworth It's a Pleasure. In particolours, she has several winners from Travis and Craigleith lines.

Brit and Jostein Halvorsen's Bomway kennel started with Hubbestads and Lochranza lines. Their latest winners are Ch. Bomway Safe Landing and Ch. Bomway Secret Combination (by Ch. Bidston Solomon).

SWEDEN
In Sweden, Gerd Pedersen's Hubbestad Cockers won well with her beautiful imports

Leavenworth Paper Tiger: Cocker of the Year in Finland 1994; owned by Anja Puumala.

Ch. Bidston Solomon. Bred by Mrs V. Hillary (GB), owned by Anja Puumala (Finland).

from Lochranza, Kenavon and Lochdene kennels. She is not breeding Cockers any more. Kari Haave-Johnsson with her Travis kennel is behind almost every winner in Sweden and Norway. Her particolours are mostly from the Celeste of Helenwood–Deewell Senator combination. Nowadays, mixed together with red Ch. Leavenworth It's a Pleasure, she has produced top black winners.

Lillemor Boos' Greentree Cockers started with Travis particolours and solids. Nowadays, mixed with Leavenworth breeding, she has produced really beautiful solid winners.

Inger Ekwall's Liecocks Cockers have good particolours from Travis lines mated to Keegan's Glory of Coltrim.

FINLAND

In Finland my own solid Leavenworth Cockers are certainly behind many winners in Scandinavia. My latest winner is Leavenworth Paper Tiger (by Leavenworth Hold that Tiger [by Solomon from a Leavenworth Tradition daughter]). He became Cocker of the Year 1994.

In the 1980s Anne and Airi Moki won a great deal with their Pounikaon Cockers. At the present time they breed very few litters a year.

From the Pounikon dogs, Tuija Kaipainen's Sheerclever kennel has developed and she wins very well nowadays. She has imported several dogs from the Charbonnel kennel in England.

Nina Kauhanen's Northworth Cockers started with Leavenworth dogs and she has also successfully used Tanac's Play It Again.

In particolours, Pirjo Lehtanen's Breeze kennel imported several dogs from the Courtmaster, Lindridge, Weirdene and Kendalwood kennels in the UK bloodlines.

From Breeze dogs, Mariann and Markenn Korpi started their Benchmark Cockers.

Teija Poikolainen, owner of the Crawford Cockers, owned the big winner of the 1980s, Harwenprince Evening Star. Nowadays, she has imported several dogs from Lynwater kennels.

Braz. Grand Ch. Kavora Rodeo (Sh. Ch. Platonstown Look Who I Am – Kavora Evensong): BoB World Show Argentina 1993. Bred by Miss P. Trotman, owned by Mrs S. Grant.

Argentine Grand Ch. Hollywoodde Infiesta: BIS Cocker Club Of Argentina Ch. Show 1994.

SOUTH AMERICA

I have also found the enthusiasm of Cocker people in Argentina and Uruguay to be tremendously heartening. They have had British imports of high quality as well as dogs from North America. There is a slight tendency towards the American type in some of the exhibits. I suppose that this is quite natural in view of the placings of some of the American judges who go there, but I know that dedicated officers of the Cocker Spaniel Clubs in both countries will not allow the general type to depart from the true British and FCI type.

It was also interesting to know that English judge Ron Bradbury made a seven-year-old British-bred red dog, Kavora Rodeo, Best of Breed at the World Show in Argentina in 1993. Rodeo was bred by Pam Trotman, sired by Sheila Sadler's Sh. Ch. Platonstown Look Who I Am, and owned by Susan Grant of Brazil. Mrs Grant, recently in England, took back with her Sheila Sadler's CC-winning black dog, Platonstown Rock-On Tommy. She must have been delighted when, at his first two shows, he took Best of Breed and No.4 in the Group at one, and the following day took Best of Breed and No.1 in the Group, and ended up Reserve Best in Show.

Chapter Eleven

CHAMPIONS AND SHOW CHAMPIONS 1969 – 1995

**BLUE ROAN
CHAMPIONS**

OUAINE CHIEFTAIN, Ch. D, born l.2.68, Crackshill Tricolour of Ide–Ouaine Panderosa. Br/owner, Mrs E. J. Caddy.

SCOLYS STARDUSTER, Ch. D, born 11.2.65, Goldenfields Minstrel Boy–Scolys Sweet Solera. Br/owner, Mrs D.M. Schofield.

CRETOKA ALFREDO, Ch. D, born 11.10.68, Ch. Scolys Starduster–Cretoka Marigold. Br/owner, Mrs K. Creamer.

LIGHT MUSIC OF LUCKLENA, Ch. D, born 29.7.7l, Sh. Ch. Courtdale Flag Lieutenant–Lucklena Merry Music. Br, Mrs R. Gibbs. Owner, Mr A. S. Mansfield.

SCOLYS SHOWPIECE, Ch. B, born 17.6.70, Sh. Ch. Courtdale Flag Lieutenant–Scolys Silver Laughter. Br/owner, Mrs D. M. Schofield.

BOURNEHOUSE STARSHINE, Ch. B, born 24.5.7l, Ch. Scolys Starduster–Merrybray Marie Celeste. Br/owner, Mr G. F. Williams.

SILVER MUSIC OF LUCKLENA, Ch. B, born 10.11.73, Ch. Light Music of Lucklena–Scolys Snowdrift. Br, Mrs D. J. Staton. Owner, Mr A. S. Mansfield.

LUCKLENA MINSTREL, Ch. D, born 25.9.79, Ronfil Remezzo–Ch. Silver Music of Lucklena. Br/owner, Mr A. S. Mansfield.

BOWISKEY BOY BLUE, Ch. D, born 2.6.88, Sh. Ch. Lindridge Venture–Normanview Silver Locket of Bowiskey. Brs/owners, Mr and Mrs D. Bowkis.

OKELL OUTWARD BOUND, Ch. D, born 23.9.89, Sh. Ch. Dearnewood Star Venture–Okell Onestep. Br/owner, Miss J. Walker.

BOWISKEY ISLAND BOY, Ch. D, born 27.10.91, Mistfall Meddler–Larochelle Island Girl of Bowiskey. Brs/owners, Mr and Mrs D. Bowkis.

SHOW CHAMPIONS

THE MATAROA OF MERRYBRAY, Sh. Ch. D, born 5.2.67, Sh. Ch. Courtdale Flag Lieutenant–Merrybray Honeysuckle. Br/Owners, Mr G. and Miss P. Dunn.

HIGHTREES GUNSMOKE, Sh. Ch. D, born 18.4.66, Hightrees Dusty Miller–Hightrees Pearl Blush. Br, Mr J. Gillespie. Owner, Mrs E. Ridout.

WEDGWOOD OF WEIRDENE, Sh. Ch. B, born 25.5.67, Welded Link of Weirdene–Wong Sue of Weirdene. Br/owner, Mr R. Weir.

WHATMORE OF WEIRDENE, Sh. Ch. D, born l6.4.68, Weirdene Lochranza Pearl Diver–Woodcote Honey of Weirdene. Br/owner, Mr R. Weir.

LEABANK LIMERICK, Sh. Ch. B, born 12.12.67, Leabank Luckstone–Leabank Love in a Mist. Br/owner, Mrs M. Stevens.

SCOLYS SPINNING WATER OF DIGBROW, Sh. Ch. B, born 6.11.69, Ch. Ouaine Chieftain–Scolys Silver Laughter. Br, Mrs D.M. Schofield. Owners, Mr and Mrs J.E. Brown.

PEASEMORE PLAYGOER, Sh. Ch. D, born 3.8.69, Peasemore Blue Peter–Peasemore Prelude. Br/owner, Miss M. Annetts.

STARTIME OF GLENCORA, Sh. Ch. D, born 15.3.71, Sh. Ch. Glencora Gallant Star–Rosecourt Raindrop. Br, Miss J. Wilson. Owner, Mr J. Auld.

ASQUANNE'S KIM SUPERBE, Sh. Ch. B, born 9.7.66, Lucklena Roydwood Recorder–Merry of Brenshu. Br/owner, Mrs A. Webster.

ROSECOURT REVERIE, Sh. Ch. B, born 25.6.69, Sh. Ch. Moyhill Maxwelton–Rosecourt Sealrock Sapphire. Br/owner, Miss J. G. Wilson.

MERRYWORTH MR. CHIPS, Sh. Ch. D, born l2.11.7l, Ouaine Gustav–Merryworth Maggie May. Br/owner, Mrs E.F. Chadwick.

COCHISE CZARDAS, Sh. Ch. D, born 7.3.70, Ch. Ouaine Chieftain–Sh. Ch. Cochise Circe. Brs/owners, Lt Cdr and Mrs H. Blake.

RAMIRO OF RONFIL, Sh. Ch. D, born 7.3.74, Yardew Constellation–Ronfil Rhaiwen of Colene. Br, Mrs I. White. Owner, Mrs T.M. Bebb.

BITCON BLUE MODEL, Sh. Ch. B, born 24.11.72, Sh. Ch. Leabank Levity–Hightrees Love Serenade. Br/owner, Mr M. Armstrong.

BLENKARN CLAUDIO OF COCHISE, Sh. Ch. D, born l4.2.74, Sh. Ch. Cochise Czardas–Blenkarn Blue Star. Br, Mrs B.W. Hodgetts. Owners, Lt Cdr and Mrs H. Blake.

LEABANK LEVITY, Sh. Ch. D, born 28.11.70, Ch. Scolys Starduster–Sh. Ch. Leabank Limerick. Br/owner, Mrs M. Stevens.
BOURNEHOUSE SHINE ON, Sh. Ch. B, born 3.4.74, Sh. Ch. Merryworth Mr Chips–Ch. Bournehouse Starshine. Br/owner, Mr G.F. Williams.

BITCON BLUE BERRY OF MOSSDEW, Sh. Ch. B, born 26.10.73, Sh. Ch. Leabank Levity–Hightrees Love Serenade. Br, Mr M. Armstrong. Owners, Mr and Mrs A. Moody.

STYVECHALE STARTIME, Sh. Ch. B, born 17.10.73, Aust. Ch. Scolys Strike Lucky–Styvechale Sleighbells. Br/owner, Mrs P. M. Masters.

NORMANVIEW THUNDERCLOUD, Sh. Ch. D, born 2.7.72, Normanview Silver Waters–Normanview Silver Salver. Brs/owners, Mr and Mrs J. R. Baldwin.

BITCON SILVER MODEL, Sh. Ch. B, born 5.11.75, Ch. Scolys Starduster–Sh. Ch. Bitcon Blue Model. Br/owner, Mr M. Armstrong.

BOURNEHOUSE SILVER STAR, Sh. Ch. B, born 3.4.73, Sh. Ch. Merryworth Mr Chips–Ch. Bournehouse Starshine. Br, Mr G. Williams. Owner, Mr J. Oulton.

RANEYL LATE SUMMER OF LEABANK, Sh. Ch. B, born 31.8.73, Sh. Ch. Leabank Levity–Raneyl Pretty Miss. Br, Mr F. Salisbury. Owner, Mrs M. Stevens.

COLTRIM CRACKERJACK OF TARLING, Sh. Ch. D, born 3.2.74, Ch. Scolys Starduster–Nostrebor Nonsense. Brs, Mr and Mrs A. E. Simpson. Owner, Mrs O. Norfolk.

NORMANVIEW SCOTS GREY, Sh. Ch. D, 26.9.75, Normanview Thunderstrike of Merrybray–Normanview Nightingale. Brs/owners, Mr and Mrs J. R. Baldwin.

WESTDYKE WEEL KENT MAN, Sh. Ch. D, born 15.5.78, Sh. Ch. Chrisolin Cambiare of Styvechale–Westdyke Wise Words. Br/owner, Mr W. Robertson.

BITCON RHAPSODY, Sh. Ch. B, born 20.5.78, Sh. Ch. Ramiro of Ronfil–Sh. Ch. Bitcon Blue Model. Br/owner, Mr M. Armstrong.

BITCON FLORIN OF MISTFALL, Sh. Ch. B, born 29.10.77, Sh. Ch. Leabank Levity–Renanda Love Story. Br, Mr M. Armstrong. Owner, Mr G. Parkin.

DAVOREY LUCKY SENTINEL, Sh. Ch. D, born 17.5.77, Davorey Charlie George–Emma Jane of Hightrees. Br/owner, Mrs Pykett.

WILHOLME WALTZTIME, Sh. Ch. B, born 2.9.76, Helenwood Firecrest–Wilholme Witchcraft. Br/owner, Mr D. Shields.

BITCON BABYCHAM, Sh. Ch. B, born 7.2.79, Hightrees Sweet Talk of Lochranza–Renanda Love Story. Br/owner, Mr M. Armstrong.

WEIRDENE WONDERFUL ONE, Sh. Ch. B, born 17.8.77, Weirdene Worthy Friend–Weirdene Westerly Sunset. Br/owner, Mr R. Weir.

CILLEINE ECHELON, Sh. Ch. D, born 18.2.80, Hightrees Sweet Talk of Lochranza–Styvechale Stardew of Cilleine. Br/owner, Mrs D. M. Barney.

COCHISE CHIRICAHUA, Sh. Ch. D, born 2.1.79, Harwenprince Sonata–Cochise Caparica. Brs/owners, Lt Cdr and Mrs H. Blake.

COCHISE CSHAKIRA, Sh. Ch. B, born 2.1.79, Harwenprince Sonata–Cochise Caparica. Brs/owners, Lt Cdr and Mrs H. Blake.

RICHBET SNOWFALL OF MATTERHORN, Sh. Ch. B, born 1.4.79, Matterhorn Masterpiece–Galen Loving Words. Br, Mr R. A. Lewis. Owner, Mr H. M. Jones.

COLINWOOD BELLBOY, Sh. Ch. D, born 27.9.78, Frant Blue Stone–Colinwood Rhapsody. Brs/owners, Mr and Mrs P. C. Woolf.

DEARNEWOOD STAR VENTURE, Sh. Ch. D, born 7.6.78, Sh. Ch. Leabank Levity–Scolys Silver Cygnet. Brs/owners, Mr and Mrs R. Richardson.

MISTFALL MOOD INDIGO, Sh. Ch. B, born 24.1.80, Sh. Ch. Dearnewood Star Venture–Snowgate Blue Lady. Br/owner, Mr G. Parkin.

CHRISOLIN MOONLIGHT MAGIC OF CLASSICWAY, Sh. Ch. B, born 5.4.78, Falconers Envoy of Ware–Chrisolin Cantata. Br, Mrs C.M. Gardner. Owners, Mr and Mrs E. W. Darby.

LINDRIDGE LUCKY CHARM, Sh. Ch. B, born 9.7.81, Sh. Ch. Cilleine Echelon–Sh. Ch. Lindridge Silver Charm. Br/owner, Mrs A. Hackett.

OUAINE JURYMAN, Sh. Ch. D, born 26.6.79, Ouaine Diogenes–Ouaine Santa Rosa. Br/owner, Mrs E. J. Caddy.

COLTRIM MISSISSIPPI GAMBLER, Sh. Ch. D, born 17.12.80, Matterhorn Masterpiece–Coltrim Dakota Sioux. Brs/owners, Mr and Mrs A. E. Simpson.

ASQUANNE'S OMEN, Sh. Ch. D, born 2.9.81. Commander of Courtdale–Asquanne's Leanne. Brs/owners, Mr and Mrs A. Webster.

LINDRIDGE SILVER CHARM, Sh. Ch. B, born 31.5.78, Sh. Ch. Chrisolin Cambiare of Styvechale–Lindridge Spot On. Br/owner, Mrs A. Hackett.

BITCON HOT GOSSIP, Sh. Ch. B, born 6.12.80, Bitcon Silver Rebel–Renanda Love Story. Br/owner, Mr M. Armstrong.

CLASSICWAY CROCUS TIME, Sh. Ch. B, born 14.9.81, Sh. Ch. Cilleine Echelon–Adargi Joyful Girl of Classicway. Brs/owners, Mr and Mrs E. W. Darby.

SHANAZ SHORT AND SWEET, Sh. Ch. B, born 24.9.81, Hightrees Sweet Talk of Lochranza–Sapphire of Shanaz. Br/owner, Mrs W. Reid.

MISTFALL MANDALAY, Sh. Ch. B, born 9.6.82, Bitcon Silver Rebel–Sh. Ch. Mistfall Mood Indigo. Br/owner, Mr G. Parkin.

LINDRIDGE GYPSY GIRL, Sh. Ch. B, born 13.8.83, Styvechale Storm Cloud–Sh. Ch. Lindridge Silver Charm. Br/owner, Mrs A. Hackett.

HARADWAITHE SORCERESS, Sh. Ch. B, born 11. 11. 82, Haradwaithe Quickstep–Mistfall Moviestar of Haradwaithe. Brs/owners, Mr S. E. Clayforth and Mr R. Peters.

TUDORGOLD NIMROD VARIATIONS FROM MAXWAY, Sh. Ch. D, born 22.6.83, Sh. Ch. Coltrim Mississippi Gambler–Tudorgold Raindrop Prelude. Br, Miss O. M. Tennant. Owner, Mr K. McFarlane.

CLASSICWAY CARRIE ANN, Sh. Ch. B, born 14.9.81, Sh. Ch. Cilleine Echelon–Adargi Joyful Girl of Classicway. Brs/owners, Mr and Mrs E. W. Darby.

COURTMASTER JE SUIS, Sh. Ch. B, born 1.10.81., Sh. Ch. Cilleine Echelon–Wild Oats of Ware. Brs/owners Mr D. and Mrs S. Telford.

OKELL OLE, Sh. Ch. B, born 23.7.81, Sh. Ch. Colinwood Bellboy–Shielwood Crown Jewel of Okell. Br/owner, Miss J. Walker.

CLASSICWAY CONCORDE, Sh. Ch. D, born 24.1.85, Normanview Midnight Runner of Classicway–Classicway Candice of Sudawn. Br, Mrs S. D. Eaton. Owners, Mr and Mrs E. W. Darby.

BLUE ROAN

Sh. Ch. Lindridge Gypsy Girl. Owned by Mrs A. Hackett.
Photo: Roger Chambers.

Sh. Ch. Ouaine Juryman. Owned by Mrs J. Caddy.

Sh. Ch. Classicway Catch A Star. Owned by Mr & Mr E. Darby.

Sh. Ch. Shanaz Short List. Owned by Mrs W. Reid.

NORMANVIEW STORMTROUPER, Sh. Ch. D, born 18.11.81, Normanview Blue Rondo–Normanview Night Lady. Brs, Mr J. and Mrs D. Baldwin. Owners, Mr and Mrs J. L. Reid.

KENDRA HARMONY CHILD, Sh. Ch. B, born 24.9.82, Styvechale Stormcloud–Kendra Graceful Child. Brs/owners, Mr and Mrs K. Morrisson.

CLASSICWAY CHARMAINE, Sh. Ch. B, born 16.10.83, Normanview Midnight Runner of Classicway–Sh. Ch. Classicway Carrie Ann. Brs, Mr and Mrs E. W. Darby. Owners, Mr and Mrs J. Perry.

SQUIRESBROOK ELECTRA, Sh. Ch. B, born 13.12.82, Bowerleas Braemore of Laicsyde–Styvechale Sainete. Br, Mrs D.J. Staton. Owner, Mrs S. M. Jones.

MOSSDEW IMAGINATION, Sh. Ch. B, born 4.9.82, Sh. Ch. Cillcine Echelon–Wyrepark Passing Fancy. Brs, Mr and Mrs A. Moody. Owner, Mr R. W. Jackson.

BITCON SHY TALK, Sh. Ch. B, born 20.7.84, Mistfall Meddler–Bitcon Artists Model. Br/owner, Mr M. Armstrong.

WILHOLME WRANGLER, Sh. Ch. D, born 4.9.82, Styvechale Stormcloud–Wilholme Who Loves Ya Baby. Br, Mr D. W. Shields. Owner, Mrs S. Shields.

ASQUANNE'S COUGAN AT SUNDEALA, Sh. Ch. D, born 7.3.85, Sh. Ch. Asquanne's Omen–Cascade at Derlan. Brs, Mr and Mrs A. Webster. Owners, Mrs B. E. Davies and Mr R. Bebb.

COURTMASTER ABRACADABRA, Sh. Ch. D, born 23.5.85, Normanview Midnight Runner of Classicway–Courtmaster Santa Lucia. Brs/owners, Mr and Mrs D. J. Telford.
MAXWAY MUSIC MAKER, Sh. Ch. D, born 9.7.84, Sh. Ch. Tudorgold Nimrod Variations from Maxway–Orange Meringue from Maxway. Br/owner, Mr K. McFarlane.

LINDRIDGE VENTURE, Sh. Ch. D, born 29.10.85, Mistfall Meddler–Sh. Ch. Lindridge Gypsy Girl. Br/owner, Mrs A. Hackett.

CLASSICWAY CRESSIDA, Sh. Ch. B, born 12.7.84, Sh. Ch. Cilleine Echelon–Adargi Joyful Girl of Classicway. Brs/owners, Mr and Mrs E. W. Darby.

Sh. Ch. Towbray Tosca. Owned by Mrs H. Ladanowski.

Sh. Ch. Classicway Clippers Dream Of Cosalta. Owned by Mr & Mrs P. & Miss S. Swigciski.

Sh. Ch. Mistfall Moet. Owned by Mr F. Whyte.

Sh. Ch. Cassom April Sky. Owned by Miss S. Amos Jones.

TOWBRAY TOSCA, Sh. Ch. B, born 3.8.84, Bowerleas Braemore of Laicsyde–Towbray Sweet Surprise. Br/owner, Mrs H. Ladanowski.

LADLOR SOUL MATE, Sh. Ch. D, born 20.10.87, Haradwaithe Specialist–Soul Train to Ladlor. Br/owner, Mrs L. Nobes.

BLENCARN BASSANIO, Sh. Ch. D, born 9.3.84, Sh. Ch. Cilleine Echelon–Blenkarn Dolly Blue. Br/owner, Mrs B. Hodgetts.

ZAMS SILVER DOLLAR, Sh. Ch. D, born 11.7.83, Ouaine Rockefeller–Ouaine Honeysuckle of Zams. Br, Mrs P. J. Lindsay. Owners, Mr K. J. Harwood and Mr M. J. Masters.

REMOLA ZOLA AT DEARNEWOOD, Sh. Ch. B, born 13.3.87, Sh. Ch. Dearnewood Star Venture–Remola Vivacity. Br, Mr F. E. Millward. Owners, Mr and Mrs R. Richardson.

BITCON SHAWNE, Sh. Ch. B, born 4.6.85, Mistfall Meddler–Sh. Ch. Bitcon Babycham. Br/owner, Mr M. Armstrong.

CLASSICWAY CAT'S WHISKERS, Sh. Ch. B, born 30.10.85, Normanview Midnight Runner of Classicway–Sh. Ch. Classicway Carrie Ann. Brs, Mr and Mrs E. W. Darby. Owner, Mrs D. Darby.

OKELL OVATION, Sh. Ch. B, born 5.11.84, Okell Ovett–Okell Oracle. Br/owner, Miss J. Walker.

CLASSICWAY CUTTY SARK, Sh. Ch. D, born 25.12.87, Oldberrow Scorched Earth of Coppynook–Gemland Out of the Blue of Classicway. Brs/owners, Mr and Mrs E. W. Darby.

MIDNIGHT BLUE HORIZON OF CLASSICWAY, Sh. Ch. D, born 1.10 86, Normanview Midnight Runner of Classicway–Blue Foxy Lady at Joaldy. Br, Mrs J. Pretty. Owners, Mr and Mrs E. W. Darby.

SOFUS INTERVENTION, Sh. Ch. D, born 8.7.86, Weirdene Winning Hand–Murbrackans Morning Myth of Sofus. Br, Mrs G. Lindquist. Owner, Mr J. Hyslop.

LINDRIDGE VANITY FAIR, Sh. Ch. B, born 7.1.88, Sh. Ch. Lindridge Venture–Sh. Ch. Lindridge Lucky Charm. Br/owner, Mrs A. Hackett.

BITCON MOONLIGHT, Sh. Ch. B, born 25.5.87, Bitcon After Dark–Bitcon Blue Cascade. Br/owner, Mr M. Armstrong.

DAWN CHORUS OF DIALYNNE AT MATTERHORN, Sh. Ch. B, born 14.8.86, Woodbine Tobias–Adnams Fleckle Face. Brs, Mr and Mrs Melton. Owners, Miss D. Spavin and Mr H. Jones.

SALABAH SAVANNA, Sh. Ch. B, born 30.8.87, Sh. Ch. Cilleine Echelon–Normanview Moonshine of Zebec. Br/owners, Messrs M. Roberts and W. Hopkins.

BITCON PACIFIC BLUE, Sh. Ch. D, born 15.7.88, Ouaine Silver Buck–Sh. Ch. Bitcon Shy Talk. Br/owner, Mr M. Armstrong.

CLASSICWAY COUNTRY LIFE OF KENDALWOOD, Sh. Ch. D, born 22.1.87, Normanview Midnight Runner of Classicway–Sh. Ch. Classicway Carrie Ann. Brs, Mr and Mrs E. W. Darby. Owners, Mr and Mrs R. Wyatt.

LYNWATER FORGET ME NOT, Sh. Ch. B, born 1.8.87, Quasar Zodiac–Lynwater Wallflower. Br/owner, Mrs E. Maclean.

BITCON TROUBADOR, Sh. Ch. D, born 4.8.89, Mistfall Meddler–Sh. Ch. Bitcon Moonlight. Br, Mr M. Armstrong. Owner, Mrs K. Armstrong.

COURTDALE MR MAGIC, Sh. Ch. D, born 3.11.89, Sh. Ch. Lindridge Salute–Courtmaster Jezebel. Brs/owners, Mr and Mrs D. Telford.

EWTOR COOL CUSTOMER, Sh. Ch. D, born 19.3.90, Ewtor Back Scratcher–Ewtor Secret Combination. Br/owner, Mr A. D. Moss.

CARON CARBO BOOSTER, Sh. Ch. D, born 3.6.88, Sh. Ch. Coltrim Cincinatti–Courtmaster Jenny Wren. Brs/owners, Dr and Mrs J. E. Jones.

LINDRIDGE SALUTE, Sh. Ch. D, born 14.4.88, Starchoice of Lindridge–Sh. Ch. Lindridge Gypsy Girl. Br/owner, Mrs A. Hackett.

SHANAZ SHORT LIST, Sh. Ch. D, born 2.10.88, Flashlight at Shanaz–Shanaz Solitaire. Br/owner, Mrs W. Reid.

ANGMOR MINUET, Sh. Ch. B, born 18.9.86, Mistfall Meddler–Angmor Fantasia. Br/owner, Mrs J. Tinley.

OKELL OPTIMISM, Sh. Ch. B, born 23.7.88, Kendra Son of Okell–Okell Ovetta. Br/owner, Miss J. Walker.

DIALYNNE SENATOR OF SALABAH, Sh. Ch. D, born 9.5.91, Admiral Benbow at Clarksland of Dialynne–Sh. Ch. Dawn Chorus of Dialynne at Matterhorn. Brs, Miss D. Spavin and Mr S. C. Milner. Owners, Messrs M. Roberts and W. Hopkins.

BITCON MAKE BELIEVE, Sh. Ch. D, born 22.8.89, Sh. Ch. Bitcon Pacific Blue–Bitcon Free & Easy. Br/owner, Mr M. Armstrong.

Matterhorn Montage, Sh. Ch. D, born 9.5.90, Sh. Ch. Coltrim Cincinnati–Matterhorn Mrs Miniver. Br/owner, Mr H. M. Jones.

BITCON MOONLIGHT MEMORIES, Sh. Ch. B, born 21.9.89, Sh. Ch. Bitcon Pacific Blue–Bitcon Butter Candy. Br, Mr M. Armstrong. Owner, Mrs K. Armstrong.

CILLEINE EULOGY, Sh. Ch. D, born 23.12.90, Sh. Ch. Cilleine Echelon–Bitcon Pollyflinders of Cilleine. Br/owner, Mrs D. M. Barney.

LINDRIDGE TOP GUN, Sh. Ch. D, born 16.9.90, Starchoice of Lindridge–Sh. Ch. Lindridge Vanity Fair. Br/owner, Mrs A. Hackett.

CLASSICWAY CATCH A STAR, Sh. Ch. B, born 26.1.92, Sh. Ch.

Classicway Country Life of Kendalwood–Lochdene Giggles of Classicway. Br/owners, Mr and Mrs E. W. Darby.

SALABAH SILVER SECRET, Sh. Ch. B, born 17.5.92, Sh. Ch. Dialynne Senator of Salabah–Salabah Silver Spirit. Br/owners, Messrs M. Roberts and W. Hopkins.

CLASSICWAY CLIPPERS DREAM OF COSALTA, Sh. Ch. D, born 13.5.91, Wilholme Commanche Run of Classicway–Bullpark Donnabella of Classicway. Br, Miss J. Darby. Owners, Mr and Mrs P. and Miss S. Swigciski.

MISTFALL MOET, Sh. Ch. B, born 4.9.92, Sh. Ch. Bitcon Troubador–Bitcon Lilac Wine. Br, Mr G. Parkin. Owner, Mr F. Whyte.

CASSOM APRIL SKY, Sh. Ch. B, born 1.4.93, Sh. Ch. Bitcon Troubador–Bitcon Bo Peep. Br/owner, Miss S. Amos Jones.

PALACECRAIG GO WEST, Sh. Ch. D, born 29.4.91, Glowhill Apollo Severn–Palacecraig Be Fair. Br/owner, Mrs S. Fleming.

SPINNEYHILL STORMY WEATHER OVER FONESSE, Sh. Ch. D, born 27.5.93, Lynwater Bouncer of Spinneyhill–Spinneyhill Sense of Rhythm. Br, Mr P. J. Morgan. Owners, Mr J. and Mrs F. Mace.

SHENMORE SEEING STARS, Sh. Ch. B, born 11.11.92, Sh. Ch. Bitcon Troubador–Shenmore Starlet. Brs/owners, Mr A. Jones and Ms J. E. Simmonds.

BLUE ROAN AND TAN
NONE

BLACK AND WHITE
SHOW CHAMPIONS

COCHISE CZOLOUSHKA, Sh. Ch. B, born 25.11.71 Ouaine Gustav–Sh. Ch. Cochise Circe. Brs/owners, Lt Cdr and Mrs H. Blake.

DELSTAR OF DIGBROW, Sh. Ch. B, born 22.11.71, Ch. Scolys Starduster–Sh. Ch. Scolys Spinning Water of Digbrow. Brs/owners, Mr and Mrs J. E. Brown.

CHRISOLIN CAMBIARE OF STYVECHALE, Sh. Ch. D, born 2.1.74, Aust. Ch. Scolys Strike Lucky–Chrisolin Cantata. Br, Mrs C. Gardner. Owner, Mrs P. M. Masters.

SERENADER OF STYVECHALE, Sh. Ch. D, Born 25.8.75, Sh. Ch. Chrisolin Cambiare of Styvechale–Styvechale Silver Leaf of Hobmoor. Br, Mr D. Worrall. Owner, Mrs P. Masters.

MATTERHORN MANHATTAN, Sh. Ch. D, born 24.10.78, Sh. Ch. Chrisolin Cambiare of Styvechale–Matterhorn Masquerade. Br/owner, Mr H. M. Jones.

MATTERHORN MICK THE MILLER, Sh. Ch. D, born 28.1.81, Coltrim Confederate of Craigleith–Matterhorn Masquerade. Br/owner, Mr H. M. Jones.

MATTERHORN MONTANA, Sh. Ch. D, born 7.7.82, Sh. Ch. Matterhorn Mick the Miller–Sh. Ch. Richbet Snowfall of Matterhorn. Br/owner, Mr H. M. Jones.

MATTERHORN MORNING MIST, Sh. Ch. B, born 9.6.83, Sh. Ch. Matterhorn Montana–Matterhorn Madrigal. Br/owner, Mr H. M. Jones.

COLTRIM CINCINNATI, Sh. Ch. D, born 13.1.87, Sh. Ch. Coltrim Mississippi Gambler–Lochdene Lavender of Coltrim. Br/owners, Mr and Mrs A. E. Simpson.

BLACK & WHITE
Sh. Ch. Coltrim Cincinnatti. Bred by Mr & Mrs E.A. Simpson, owned by Miss D. Mason (USA).

LIVER/CHOCOLATE ROAN
Sh. Ch. Sprogmore Sachmo. Owned by Mrs A. Moore.

Photo: T. Morgan.

BLACK, WHITE AND TAN
SHOW CHAMPIONS

PENTAVY RIVER PATROL, Sh. Ch. D, born 27.9.69, Ch. Ouaine Chieftain–Pentavy Prairie Rose. Br/owner, Mrs K. G. Holmes.

GLENCORA FOXGLOVE, Sh. Ch. B, born 27.3.69, Glencora Game One–Confetti of Charmace. Br/owner, Mr J. Auld.

OUAINE CHIPAWAY, Sh. Ch. D, born 11 11.72, Waylight of Weirene–Ouaine Panderosa. Br/owner, Mrs E. J. Caddy.

LIVER/CHOCOLATE ROAN
SHOW CHAMPIONS

SPROGMORE SACHMO, Sh. Ch. D, born 7.4.87, Oldberrow Blue Charm–Oldberrow Chocolate Sundae of Sprogmore. Br/owner, Mrs A. Moore.

LIVER/CHOCOLATE ROAN AND TAN
NONE

LIVER/CHOCOLATE AND WHITE
NONE

LIVER/CHOCOLATE, WHITE AND TAN
NONE

ORANGE ROAN
SHOW CHAMPIONS

WAIT FOR ME OF WEIRENE, Sh. Ch. B, born 17.8.70, Sh. Ch. Whatmore of Weirene–Why Tell of Weirene. Br/owner, Mr R. Weir.

MERRYBRAY MONTANA, Sh. Ch. B, born 5/8/75, Mandate of Merrybray–Merrybray My Gem. Brs/owners, Mr G. and Miss P. Dunn.

ORANGE AND WHITE
SHOW CHAMPIONS

KIRKDON PEACHES 'N' CREAM, Sh. Ch. B, born 24.9.72,

Cochise Casimir–Kirkdon Orange Sparkle. Br/owner, Mr T. E. W. Heavisides.

PANDOREK CRISPIN, Sh. Ch. D, born 24.8.79, Coltrim Confederate of Craigleith–Pandorek Pattimac. Br/owner, Mrs P. Mace.

CRAIGLEITH THE WALTZ DREAM, Sh. Ch. B, born 14.1.78, Craigleith The Waltz King–Craigleith Candy Kisses. Br/owner, Mrs M. Robinson.

COLTRIM MYSTIC WARRIOR, Sh. Ch. D, born 30.6.86, Lochdene Ping Pong of Coltrim–Coltrim Dakota Sioux. Brs/owners, Mr and Mrs A. E. Simpson.

LYNWATER DAWN SHIMMER, Sh. Ch. B, born 7.7.9l, Lynwater Tiger Moth–Night Escapade of Lynwater. Br/owner, Mrs E. Maclean.

BLACK
SHOW CHAMPIONS

NOSLIEN NIGHT PORTER, Sh. Ch. D, born 5.3.63, Noslien Napoleon–Treetops Noslien Nandina. Br/owner, Miss P. Neilson.

MERRYBORNE SIMONE, Sh. Ch. B, born 8.6.67, Sh. Ch. Lochranza Quettadenes Marksman–Lochranza Honey Glow. Br/owner, Mrs I. Martin.

LOCHRANZA BITTERSWEET, Sh. Ch. B, born 29.5.66, Sh. Ch. Lochranza Quettadenes Marksman–Lochranza Monkspring Marigold. Br/owner, Miss J. Macmillan.

LOCHRANZA PEELERS LEGAL LOVE, Sh. Ch. B, born 12.8.66, Sh. Ch. Lochranza Quettadenes Marksman–Sh. Ch. Eldwythe Mornessa Milora. Br, Mrs M. France. Owner, Miss J. Macmillan.

OLANZA PIPISTRELLE, Sh. Ch. B, born 31.8.68, Butterprint of Broomleaf–Black Pansy of Andana. Br/owner, Miss P. Becker.

GOLDENFIELDS PENNY BLACK, Sh. Ch. B, born l7.9.68, Sh. Ch. Lochranza Strollaway–Goldenfields Scilla. Br, Miss D. Robinson. Owner, Mrs F. M. Wilkinson.

PLATONSTOWN BUZZARDWAY SAMBO, Sh. Ch. D, born 29.7.69, Tam O' Shanter of Sorbrook–Cholesbury Red Cinders. Br, Mr T. Sanderson. Owner, Mrs M. Snary.

LOCHRANZA SEAMILE TALKABOUT, Sh. Ch. D, born 28.6.69, Lochranza William Tell–Lochranza Evening Star. Brs, Mr and Mrs Sealey. Owner, Miss J. Macmillan.

AMANDA JANE OF SORBROOK, Sh. Ch. B, born 28.11.68, Cornbow Manfred–Quettadenes Bernadette. Brs/owners, Mr and Mrs J. Smith.

GLENCORA MEADOW PRINCE, Sh. Ch. D, born 3.8.69, Sh. Ch. Glencora Black Ace–Lochranza Meadow Sweet. Br/owner, Mr J. Auld.

VALSISSIMO OF MISBOURNE, Sh. Ch. D, born 6.3.70, Sunglint of Sorbrook–Valswych of Misbourne. Br, Miss D. M. Hahn. Owner, Mrs P. Price.

LOCHRANZA NEWSPRINT, Sh. Ch. D, born 27.3.71, Butterprint of Broomleaf–Sh. Ch. Lochranza Bittersweet. Br/owner, Miss J. Macmillan.

JANEACRE NIGHT SKIPPER OF HELENWOOD, Sh. Ch. D, born 28.7.72, Sunglint of Sorbrook–Janeacre Maid Marion of Lochnell. Brs, Mr and Mrs J. Holdsworth. Owner, Mrs J. H. Marris-Bray.

SORBROOK PLAYBOY, Sh. Ch. D, born 7.8.70, Cornbow Manfred–Fyne Lady of Sorbrook. Brs, Mr and Mrs J. Smith. Owner, Mr J. Oulton.

OLANZA PIPERS DREAM, Sh. Ch. B, born 30.5.70, Butterprint of Broomleaf–Bramclere Olanza Pipers Tune. Br, Mrs R. Warren. Owner, Miss P. Becker.

COLINWOOD FINE LACE, Sh. Ch. B, born 16.6.70, Colinwood Summerleaf of Lochnell–Colinwood Wild Thyme. Brs/owners, Mr and Mrs P. C. Woolf.

ASTRAWIN ARKADINA, Sh. Ch. B, born 25.5.70, Sunglint of Sorbrook–Sh. Ch. Astrawin Amusing. Brs/owners, Mr and Mrs S. Wise.

Benedict of Broomleaf, Sh. Ch. D, born 16.8.73, Sh. Ch. Bronze Knight of Broomleaf–Sh. Ch. Olanza Pipistrelle. Br, Miss P. Becker. Owner, Mrs K. Doxford.

HELENWOOD CHECKMATE, Sh. Ch. D, born 2.5.74, Sh. Ch. Janeacre Night Skipper of Helenwood–Helenwood Celebration. Br/owner, Mrs J. Marris-Bray.

MISBOURNE SWEET ANICE, Sh. Ch. B, born 26.12.72, Valdikler of Misbourne–Sweet Rebecca of Misbourne. Br/owner, Miss D. M. Hahn.

KONIGSEA NIGHT GLINT OF PLATONSTOWN, Sh. Ch. B, born 12.1.74, Sunglint of Sorbrook–Konigsea Karen. Br, Mr P. Bradford. Owner, Mrs M. Snary.

KENAVON ENVOY, Sh. Ch. D, born 1.7.73, Lochranza Quettadene Diplomat–Kenavon Autumn Crocus. Br, Miss B. Mingay. Owners, Mr and Mrs E. W. Darby.

RENGIL RANSY OF PLATONSTOWN, Sh. Ch. D, born 15.7.74, Sorbrook Sweet William–Rengil Renede. Br, Mr G. Wood. Owner, Mrs M. Snary.

MISBOURNE PAPER CHASE OF LOCHRANZA, Sh. Ch. D, born 29.8.74, Sh. Ch. Newsreader of Lochranza–Sweet Rebecca of Misbourne. Br, Miss D. M. Hahn. Owners, Miss J. Macmillan and Mrs J. Gillespie.

LOCHRANZA MAN OF FASHION, Sh. Ch. D, born 31.3.76, Lochranza Night to Remember–Lochranza Dolly Posh. Brs/owners, Miss J. Macmillan and Mrs J. Gillespie.

HELENWOOD CHRYSILLA, Sh. Ch. B, born 23.9.74, Sh. Ch. Janeacre Night Skipper of Helenwood–Helenwood Tanfaisie. Br/owner, Mrs J. Marris-Bray.

KAVORA BLACK PEARL OF LOCHRANZA, Sh. Ch. B, born 20.8.72, Sh. Ch. Lochranza Newsprint–Kavora Belinda. Br, Miss P. Trotman. Owners Miss J. Macmillan and Mrs J. Gillespie.

BROOMLEAF BRIGHT MEMORY, Sh. Ch. D, born 7.4.76, Sh. Ch. Benedict of Broomleaf–Butter Candy of Broomleaf. Br/owner, Mrs K. Doxford.

CILLEINE SOLDIER BOY, Sh. Ch. D, born 20.1.71, Bugle Boy of Cilleine–Kavora April Morn of Cilleine. Br/owner, Mrs D. Barney.

BLACK SILK OF BROOMLEAF, Sh. Ch. B, born 7.4.76, Sh. Ch. Benedict of Broomleaf–Butter Candy of Broomleaf. Br, Mrs K. Doxford. Owner, Miss P. Becker.

KAVORA NIGHTLIGHT, Sh. Ch. B, born 16.3.76, Sh. Ch. Janeacre Night Skipper of Helenwood–Kavora Joanna. Br/owner, Miss P. Trotman.

KONIGSEA KANKARA OF PLATONSTOWN, Sh. Ch. B, born 25.10.75, Brandy Butter of Broomleaf–Konigsea Klansee. Br, Mr P. Bradford. Owner, Mrs M. Snary.

ROCKAYDONS JET JASPER, Sh. Ch. D, born 12.6.74, Sh. Ch. Helenwood Checkmate–Rimaelia Gold Cheri. Br, M. Simms. Owner, Mrs K. Simms.

CORNBOW NIGHT OWL, Sh. Ch. D, born 15.7.74, Sh. Ch. Janeacre Night Skipper of Helenwood–Mint Toes of Cornbow. Br/owner, Mr J. Clarke.

KAVORA BLACKBIRD, Sh. Ch. D, born 12. 8. 77, Sh. Ch. Bobbinbraes Echo–Kavora Jenny Wren. Br/owner, Miss P. Trotman.

COLINWOOD WITCHCRAFT, Sh. Ch. B, born 5.10.74, Colinwood Tango–Colinwood Wood Sorrel. Brs/owners, Mr and Mrs P. Woolf.

RENGIL RENSHEEN, Sh. Ch. B, born 24.11.77, Platonstown Star Quality of Rengil–Rengil Renlibby. Br, Mr G. Wood. Owner, Mrs M. Snary.

STYVECHALE SHINE ON OF CILLEINE, Sh. Ch. B, born 18.1.78, Sh. Ch. Cilleine Soldier Boy–Styvechale Shining Shoes. Br, Mrs P. Masters. Owner, Mrs D. Barney.

MISBOURNE POSTMARK, Sh. Ch. D, born 7.7.78, Misbourne Valbengy–Sh. Ch. Misbourne Sweet Anice. Br/owner, Miss D. M. Hahn.

PLATONSTOWN SUPER DUPER, Sh. Ch. D, born 17.9.76, Sh. Ch. Rengil Ransy of Platonstown–Sh. Ch. Konigsea Night Glint of Platonstown. Br/owner, Mrs M. Snary.

LOCHRANZA BLACK ONYX, Sh. Ch. D, born 1. 12.77, Sh. Ch. Lochranza Man of Fashion–Kavora Black Pearl of Lochranza. Brs/owners, Miss J. Macmillan and Mrs J. Gillespie.

BROWSTER JONJO, Sh. Ch. D, born 4.4.78, Persuader of Browster–Browster Victorian Rose. Br/owner, Mr J. W. Tyson.

KAVORA NIGHT STAR OF OLANZA, Sh. Ch. B, born 30.9.78, Sh. Ch. Janeacre Night Skipper of Helenwood–Kavora April Star. Br, Miss P. Trotman. Owner, Miss P. Becker.

Sh. Ch. Olanza Poachers Moon. Owned by Miss P. Becker.

Sh. Ch. Canigou Mr Happy. Owned by Mrs P. Bentley.

Photo: Roger Chambers.

Sh. Ch. Sorbrook Jemrey Black Bess. Owned by Mr & Mrs J. Smith.

Sh. Ch. Canigou Patent Applied For. Owned by Mrs P. Bentley.

CILLEINE ATHENE, Sh. Ch. B, born 8.10.78, Sh. Ch. Lochranza Newsprint–Kavora April Morn of Cilleine. Br/owner, Mrs D. M. Barney.

SORBROOK BRAMBLEBERRY, Sh. Ch. D, born 24.11.78, Sh. Ch. Broomleaf Bright Memory–Sh. Ch. Sorbrook Holly Berry. Brs/owners, Mr and Mrs J. Smith.

ROSADAY SUPER TROOPER, Sh. Ch. D, born 29.7.81, Sh. Ch. Platonstown Super Duper–Misbourne Sweet Lizbie. Br/owner, Mrs S. Sadler.

QUETTADENE EMBLEM, Sh. Ch. D, born 30.4.83, Sh. Ch. Sorbrook Christmas Knight–Quettadene Fascination. Br/owner, Mrs P. M. Lester.

CORNBOW VENTURE, Sh. Ch. D, born 13.9.81, Bobbinbraes Solitaire of Cornbow–Cornbow Nightshade. Br/owner, Mr J. Clarke.

BIDSTON TOP OF THE POPS, Sh. Ch. D, born 9.9.79, Sh. Ch. Broomleaf Bright Memory–Bidston Easter Bonnet. Br, Mrs P. S. Hillary. Owner, Mrs D. M. Robson.

SORBROOK CHRISTMAS KNIGHT, Sh. Ch. D, born 24.12.81, Willowside Buffalo Bill–Sorbrook Penny Royal. Brs/owners, Mr and Mrs J. Smith.

PLATONSTOWN SCOOBY DOO, Sh. Ch. D, born 25.7.83, Sh. Ch. Platonstown Super Duper–Platonstown Nice and Easy. Br/owner, Mrs M. Snary.

HELENWOOD AVALAF, Sh. Ch. D, born 5.11.83, Sh. Ch. Broomleaf Bright Memory–Sh. Ch. Helenwood Capelle. Br/owner, Mrs J. Marris-Bray.

ROSADAY LEADING LADY, Sh. Ch. B, born 29.7.81, Sh. Ch. Platonstown Super Duper–Misbourne Sweet Lizbie. Br/owner, Mrs S. Sadler.

EILANS BLACK CHARLOTTE OF CHARBONNEL, Sh. Ch. B, born 3.1.84, Sonic Sailor of Charbonnel–Eilans Midnight Merryem. Br, Mrs E. Metcalf. Owner, Miss S. Lloyd.

CANIGOU MR HAPPY, Sh. Ch. D, born 15.6.84, Sh. Ch. Quettadene Emblem–Canigou Isabella Coral. Br/owner, Mrs P. L.Bentley.

BRIGHTGRASS BALLPOINT, Sh. Ch. B, born 12.5.82, Brightgrass Bounty–Brightgrass Bryony. Br/owner, Mrs J. Irwin.
SORBROOK SORCERESS, Sh. Ch. B, born 16.3.84, Sorbrook Charcoal–Sorbrook Jezebel. Brs/owners, Mr and Mrs J. Smith.

CANYONN CASSANDRA, Sh. Ch. B, born 7.11.84, Sh. Ch.

Sh. Ch. Olanza Prince Of Dreams At Perrytree. Owned By Mrs J. Rowland.

Sh. Ch. Asquanne's Giorgio. Owned by Mr & Mrs A. Webster.

Sh. Ch. Judika Japan Dreaming. Owned by Mr & Mrs K. Costello.

Sh. Ch. & Irish Sh. Ch. Faymyr Country Squire Of Kavala. Owned by Mr J. McDowell.

Quettadene Emblem Sh. Ch. Canyonn Christa. Br/owner, Mrs S. Young.

CURAGOWRIE CULTURE CLUB, Sh. Ch. D, born 6.10.85, Sh. Ch. Bidston Top of the Pops–Curagowrie Coquet. Br, Mrs F. Curran. Owners, Mrs F. Curran and Mrs R. Hume.

OLANZA POACHERS MOON, Sh. Ch. D, born 22.8.85, Sh. Ch. Quettadene Emblem–Olanza Princess Gem. Br/owner, Miss P. Becker.

ROANWOOD FLINT, Sh. Ch. D, born 12.9.85, Sh. Ch. Quettadene Emblem–Roanwood Isadora. Br/owner, Mrs S. Clarke.

GLADRIEN GEM SPARKLE, Sh. Ch. B, born 16.8.83, Lorjos Something Impressive of Gladrien–Fonesse Fame. Br/owner, Mrs G. Kaufman.

ASQUANNE'S GHIA, Sh. Ch. B, born 6.10.85, Sh. Ch. Quettadene Emblem–Sh. Ch. Asquanne's Genevieve. Brs/owners, Mr and Mrs A. Webster.
OLANZA PROMISE ME, Sh. Ch. B, born 22.8.85, Sh. Ch. Quettadene Emblem–Olanza Princess Gem. Br/owner, Miss P. Becker.

FONESSE SPORTSMAN OF PLATONSTOWN, Sh. Ch. D, born 27.9.85, Sh. Ch. Platonstown Super Duper–Fonesse Fresia. Br, Mrs F. Harness. Owner, Mrs M. Snary.

HELENWOOD IVANOSHON, Sh. Ch. D, born 15.12.85, Sh. Ch. Janeacre Night Skipper of Helenwood–Helenwood By Chance. Br/owner, Mrs J. H. Marris-Bray.

CANYONN CAROLINA MOON, Sh. Ch. B, born 25.7.87, Sh. Ch. Olanza Poachers Moon–Canyonn Countessa. Br/owner, Mrs S. Young.

CANYONN CASABLANCA, Sh. Ch. B, born 1.6.87, Sh. Ch. Quettadene Emblem–Sh. Ch. Canyonn Christa. Br/owner, Mrs S. Young.

QUETTADENE HARMONY, Sh. Ch. B, born 2.9.86, Sh. Ch. Quettadene Emblem–Quettadene Sunkist. Br/owner, Mrs P. M. Lester.

CHARBONNEL CHANDALIER AT DEEWHY, Sh. Ch. B, born 5.7.85, Cordura Barbaloo–Charbonnel Charlotte. Br, Miss S. Lloyd. Owners, Mr and Mrs J. Langford.

HELENWOOD HORIZON, Sh. Ch. D, born 11.8.85, Helenwood

Grittar–Helenwood Tambarilla. Br/owner, Mrs J. Marris-Bray.

KENAN RICK O' SHEA, Sh. Ch. D, born 26.1.87, Sh. Ch. Helenwood Avalaf–Dusky Dawn of Redcar. Br/owners, Mr and Mrs A. Holmes.

SPINNEYHILL SADLER, Sh. Ch. D, born 6.4.87, Sh. Ch. Quettadene Emblem–Spinneyhill Shadow. Br/owner, Mr P. J. Morgan.

TERRIDEN HAPPY TALK, Sh. Ch. D, born 21.2.87, Sh. Ch. Canigou Mr Happy–Sorbrook Shady Lady. Brs/owners, Mr and Mrs T. Gilgallon.

MARADA ELEGANT ELOUISE, Sh. Ch. B, born 14.4.87, Sh. Ch. Canigou Mr Happy–Marada Elegant Ebony Eyes. Br/owner, Mrs C. Wood.

KELLS CLANNAD, Sh. Ch. D, born 12.3.87, Cornbow Kilcashel of Kells–Kells Connemara Crystal. Br/owner, Mrs L. V. Gilmour-Wood.

WILJANA WILD 'N' WICKED, Sh. Ch. D, born 9.11.88, Fonesse Formaster–Fonesse Foreaster. Br/owner, W. Halknett.

KAVORA ORIENT EXPRESS, Sh. Ch. D, born 14.5.87, Marandis Macho Man–Kavora Starshine Express. Br/owner, Miss P. M. Trotman.

HELENWOOD FIDDLERS FREE, Sh. Ch. B, born 8.1.88, Sh. Ch. Helenwood Haymaker–Helenwood Polkadot. Br/owner, Mrs J. Marris-Bray.

ASQUANNE'S GRAINNE, Sh. Ch. B, born 24.12.88, Faymyr Chickadee Tan Spats–Asquanne's Gigi. Brs/owners, Mr and Mrs A. Webster.

CHARBONNEL FAIR CHER, Sh. Ch. B, born 20.11.88, Helenwood Sounds Familiar–Eilans Black Charlotte of Charbonnel. Br/owner, Mrs S. Platt.

SORBROOK JEMREY BLACK BESS, Sh. Ch. B, born 2.5.87, Sh. Ch. Sorbrook Christmas Knight–Sorbrook Black Dove. Br, Mrs C. Smith. Owners, Mr and Mrs J. Smith.

CANYONN CARBON COPY, Sh. Ch. D, born 24.6.89, Sh. Ch. Helenwood Avalaf–Sh. Ch. Canyonn Cassandra. Br/owner, Mrs S. Young.

HELENWOOD COUNTRY COUSIN, Sh. Ch. B, born 15.5.89, Sh. Ch. Helenwood Ivonoshon–Sh. Ch. Helenwood Fiddlers Free. Br/owner, Mrs J. H. Marris-Bray.

LOCHDENE BAGATELLE, Sh. Ch. D, born 13. 11.88, Sh. Ch. Canigou Mr Happy–Lochdene Dew Drop. Br/owner, Mrs P. G. Shaw.

QUETTADENE MODESTY, Sh. Ch. B, born 3.11.88, Quettadene Memento–Quettadene Fascination. Br/owner, Mrs P. M. Lester.

SOLORA FINE SCRUPLES, Sh. Ch. B, born 7.2.88, Sh. Ch. Kells Clannad–Fonesse Focus. Br/owner, Mrs A. M. Harkus.

CANIGOU PATENT APPLIED FOR, Sh. Ch. D, born 25.7.91, Quettadene Debonair–Crankwood Miss Happy. Br/owner, Mrs P. L. Bentley.

ASQUANNE'S GONZALES, Sh. Ch. D, born 23.3.90, Faymyr Chickadee Tan Spats–Sh. Ch. Asquanne's Ghia. Brs/owners, Mr and Mrs A. Webster.

QUETTADENE MYSTIQUE, Sh. Ch. B, born 27.1.91, Quettadene Debonair–Sh. Ch. Quettadene Harmony. Br/owner, Mrs P. M. Lester.

MARADA ELEGANT ELOISE, Sh. Ch. B, born 14.4.87, Sh. Ch. Canigou Mr Happy–Marada Elegant Ebony Eyes. Br/owner, Mrs C. Wood.

BELIGAR RAMBLER, Sh. Ch. D, born 15.9.91, Sh. Ch. Cleavehill Pot of Gold–Kelford Black Magic. Br/owner, Mrs E. Buttrick.

FAYMYR COUNTRY SQUIRE OF KAVALA, Sh. Ch. D, born 12.10.91, Black Night of Tobermore–Faymyr Jolly Time of Bolie. Br, Mrs M. F. Quigley. Owners, Mr and Mrs J. MacDowell.

OLANZA PRINCE OF DREAMS AT PERRYTREE, Sh. Ch. D, born 16.11.90, Sh. Ch. Perrytree The Dreamer–Canyonn Coppelia of Olanza. Br, Miss P. E. Becker. Owner, Mrs J. Rowland.

ASQUANNE'S GIORGIO, Sh. Ch. B, born 31 1.92, Sh. Ch. Asquanne's Gonzales–Kendrick Kandice of Asquanne. Brs/owners, Mr and Mrs A. Webster.

JUDIKA JAPAN DREAMING, Sh. Ch. B, born 17.6.92, Sh. Ch. Perrytree The Dreamer–Judika Black Japan. Brs/owners, Mr and Mrs K. Costello.

QUETTADENE DESDEMONA, Sh. Ch. B, born 7.7.90, Quettadene Debonair–Sh. Ch. Quettadene Harmony. Br/owner, Mrs P. M. Lester.

BENCLEUCHS BLIND DATE, Sh. Ch. B, born 6.3.93, Fonesse For Keeps–Marada Touch of Elegance at Bencleuch. Brs/owners, Mr and Mrs McLaren.

WINDGROVE BLACK AS NIGHT, Sh. Ch. D, born 25.10.90, Sh. Ch. Kenan Rick O' Shea–Windgrove Touch of Class. Br/owner, Mrs K. Kerr.

CANIGOU CAMBRAI, Sh. Ch. D, born 13.9.92, Sh. Ch. Cleavehill Pot of Gold–Crankwood Miss Happy. Br/owner, Mrs P. L. Bentley.

BLACK AND TAN
SHOW CHAMPIONS

SQUIRESBROOK DUET WITH FONESSE, Sh. Ch. B, born 9.3.91, Kendrick Surprise Surprise–Squiresbrook Little Madam at Kendrick. Br, Mrs D. J. Staton. Owners, Mr and Mrs J. Mace.

RED OR GOLDEN
SHOW CHAMPIONS

KAVORA MERRYBORNE SWEET MARTINI, Sh. Ch. B, born 9.11.66, Sh. Ch. Lochranza Darnclever – Merryborne Martine. Br, Mrs I. Martin. Owner, Miss P. Trotman.

SUNREEF PLEAS BE LUVERLY, Sh. Ch. B, born 9.8.66, Sh. Ch. Astrawin April Fire–Sunreef Miss Bee-Yootiful. Brs/owners, Misses M. Scarr and M. Harris.

ASTRAWIN AUTHENTIC, Sh. Ch. D, born 1.9.67, Valdoonan of Misbourne–Astrawin Antanamaria. Brs/owners, Mr and Mrs S. Wise.

MERRYBORNE BIG SHOT, Sh. Ch. D, born 8.6.67, Sh. Ch. Lochranza Quettadenes Marksman–Lochranza Honey Glow. Br/owner, Mrs I. Martin.

SCOTSWOOD WARLORD, Sh. Ch. D, born 14 10.67, Sh. Ch. Colinwood Jackdaw of Lochnell–Scotswood Flip. Br/owner, Mrs R. Bryden.

KAVORA MERRYMAKER, Sh. Ch. D, born 27.11.68, Sh. Ch. Lochranza Quettadenes Marksman–Sh. Ch. Kavora Merryborne Sweet Martini. Br/owner, Miss P. Trotman.

COLINWOOD TURTLE DOVE, Sh. Ch. B, born 10.9.67, Colinwood Summerleaf of Lochnell–Sh. Ch. Colinwood Bunting. Br, Mrs P. Woolf. Owners, Mr and Mrs P. C. Woolf.

RED OR GOLDEN

Sh. Ch. Quettadene Discretion. Owned by Mrs P. Lester.

Sh. Ch. Canyonn Celeste. Owned by Mrs S. Young.   Photo: A. Grindle.

Sh. Ch. Asquanne's Goldfinga. Owned By Mr & Mrs A. Webster.

SIXSHOT HONEYBIRD OF LOCHNELL, Sh. Ch B, born 16.9.69, Sh. Ch. Val of Lochnell–Gold Dahlia of Lochnell. Br, Mrs M. Cameron. Owner, Mrs V. Lucas-Lucas.

NOSLIEN NEVER NAUGHTY, Sh. Ch. B, born 5.9.67, Sh. Ch. Lochranza Its A Pleasure–Sh. Ch. Noslien Naughty Nineties. Br/owner, Mrs J. A. Neilson.

LIZARN LATE SUMMER MORN, Sh. Ch. B, born 18.9.69, Butterprint of Broomleaf–Lizarn New Pence. Brs/owners, Mr and Mrs A. Hall.

BRONZE KNIGHT OF BROOMLEAF, Sh. Ch. D, born 11.6.71, Sh. Ch. Scotswood Warlord–Black Frost of Broomleaf. Br/owner, Mrs K. Doxford.

LOCHDENE SORBROOK SUNDOWNER, Sh. Ch. D, born 16.4.70, Sunglint of Sorbrook–Butterkist of Sorbrook. Brs, Mr and Mrs J. Smith. Owner, Mrs P. Shaw.

SORBROOK HOLLY BERRY, Sh. Ch. B, born 27.5.71, Lochranza Quettadene Diplomat–Quettadene Bernadette. Brs/owners, Mr and Mrs J. Smith.

BURNISHED GOLD OF BRYANSBROOK, Sh. Ch. B, born 2.6.73, Sunglint of Sorbrook–Colinwood Spun Gold. Br, Mr E. Taylor. Owner, Mr B. Fosbrook.

KAVORA HI-JINX, Sh. Ch. D, born 13.7.71, Sunglint of Sorbrook–Kavora Dancing Pupil. Br/owner, Miss P. Trotman.

LOCHRANZA FARMERS BOY, Sh. Ch. D, born 22.9.73, Sh. Ch. Bronze Knight of Broomleaf–Lochranza Dairymaid. Br, Miss J. Macmillan. Owners, Miss J. Macmillan and Mrs J. Gillespie.

BOBBINBRAES ECHO, Sh. Ch. D, born 19.12.74, Sh. Ch. Quettadene Mark–Ebony Spice of Bobbinbrae. Br/owner, Mrs H. Woodhouse.

BRYANSBROOK BUTTERKISS, Sh. Ch. B, born 9.11.74, Quettadene Golden Miller of Glowhill–Bryansbrook Ebony Bloom. Brs/owners, Mr and Mrs B. Fosbrook.

SORBROOK BEECHNUT, Sh. Ch. D, born 2.8.75, Sh. Ch. Janeacre Night Skipper of Helenwood –Sorbrook Sweet Pepper. Brs/owners, Mr and Mrs J. Smith.

BURNT TOAST OF BROOMLEAF, Sh. Ch. B, born 24.9.75, Brandy Butter of Broomleaf–Bright Glint of Broomleaf. Br/owner, Mrs K. Doxford.

NOSLIEN NEBULA, Sh. Ch. D, born 15.4.76, Sh. Ch. Lochranza Farmers Boy–Noslien News Snip. Br/owner, Miss P. Neilson.

ASTRAWIN AMBERRAN, Sh. Ch. B, born 25.3.76, Astrawin April Legacy–Astrawin Alcamilla. Brs/owners, Mr and Mrs S. Wise.

BROOMLEAF BUTTER CRISP, Sh. Ch. D, born 3.1.87, Kavora Copper King of Covana–Butter Candy of Broomleaf. Br/owner, Mrs K. Doxford.

BRYANSBROOK HIGH SOCIETY, Sh. Ch. D, born 31.3.78, Sh. Ch. Lochranza Man of Fashion–Bryansbrook Butterkiss. Brs/owners, Mr and Mrs B. Fosbrook.

COGNAC OF CURAGOWRIE, Sh. Ch. D, born 15.1.76, Curagowrie Beau Brett–Braunspath Susette. Br, D. P. Kincaid. Owners, Mrs F. Curran and Mrs R. Hume.

CANIGOU MARY ISABELLA, Sh. Ch. B, born 23.5.78, Canigou Isobert–Canigou Mary Christine. Br/owner, Mrs P. Quinn.

ASTRAWIN ASUGAR, Sh. Ch. B, born 6.5.78, Brandy Butter of Broomleaf–Astrawin Adulation. Brs/owners, Mr and Mrs S. Wise.

BROOMLEAF BARLEY BREW, Sh. Ch. D, born 21.6.78, Brandy Butter of Broomleaf–Hilgard Heidi. Brs, Mr and Mrs J. Fisher. Owner, Mrs K. Doxford.

KAVORA CHARADE, Sh. Ch. B, born 16.7.82, Sh. Ch. Broomleaf Barley Brew–Kavora Ebony Spice. Br/owner, Miss P. Trotman.

MANUCHI TOP OF THE CLASS OF KRISMOOR, Sh. Ch. D, born 27.7.82, Canigou Isobert–Kitimat Orange Princess. Brs, Mr and Mrs D. A. Guy. Owner, Miss C. J. Littlemore.

HELENWOOD AMERELLA, Sh. Ch. B, born 26.3.82, Sh. Ch. Bidston Top of the Pops–Sh. Ch. Helenwood Capelle. Br/owner, Mrs J. H. Marris-Bray.

MISBOURNE SWEET PRINCE OF PERRYTREE, Sh. Ch. D, born 30.3.85, Perrytree Gentleman Jake–Misbourne Sweet Trista. Br, Miss D. M. Hahn. Owner, Mrs J. Rowland.

CLEAVEHILL POT OF GOLD, Sh. Ch. D, born 17.3.84, Beligar Pot Black–Canyonn Christina. Br, Mrs J. M. Taylor. Owners, Mrs E. Buttrick and Mrs J. M. Taylor.

LYNWATER TAWNY OWL, Sh. Ch. B, born 1.3.82, Sh. Ch. Noslien Nebula–Lynwater Kestrel. Br/owner, Miss F. Wormell.

KAVORA NEWSMAKER, Sh. Ch. D, born 10.10.85, Kavora Newstime–Kavora Starshine Express. Br/owner, Miss P. M. Trotman.

LOCHDENE FLAMINGO OF CARDAMINE, Sh. Ch. D, born 12.11.84, Lochdene Cornelius–Lochdene Minstrel. Br, Mrs P. Shaw. Owner, Mrs P. A. Walker.

SALORA TRIVIAL PURSUITS, Sh. Ch. D, born 1. 12.84, Doves Surprise at Bidston–Fonesse Focus. Br/owner, Mrs A. Harkus.

HELENWOOD ORYELLE, Sh. Ch. B, born 6.12.85, Sh. Ch. Broomleaf Bright Memory–Sh. Ch. Helenwood Capelle. Br/owner, Mrs J. Marris-Bray.

KAVORA LUCIA, Sh. Ch. B, born 12.1.86, Kavora Hi-Fi–Kavora Bright Star. Br/owner, Miss P. Trotman.
ASTRAWIN AU RESAVOIR, Sh. Ch. B, born 17.5.85, Sh. Ch. Broomleaf Bright Memory–Astrawin Aurelia. Br/owner, Mrs P. Wise.

PLATONSTOWN LOOK WHO I AM, Sh. Ch. D, born 2.9.83, Brightgrass Brannigan–Hallbent Harriet of Platonstown. Br, Mrs M. Snary. Owner, Mrs S. Sadler.

HANLEY GEORGIA BROWN, Sh. Ch. B, born 5.4.85, Hanley Drum Major–Jonhill Peggy Sue. Brs/owners, Mr and Mrs A. Hoskins.

SNOWGATE CHRISTMAS ROSE AT MAGDALE, Sh. Ch. B, born 1. 1.87, Glowhill Gladiator of Snowgate–Special Edition to Snowgate. Br, Mrs L. Whiteley. Owner, Mr R. Dempster.

LYNWATER PEREGRINE AT BELIGAR, Sh. Ch. B, born 1.5.88, Sh. Ch. Cleavehill Pot of Gold–Sh. Ch. Lynwater Tawny Owl. Br, Miss F. Wormell. Owner, Mrs E. Buttrick.

CHATAWAY THE NEWS EDITOR, Sh. Ch. D, born 7.4.89, Broomleaf Best News–Firline Red Amber. Br/owner, Mr D. Todd.

PERRYTREE THE DREAMER, Sh. Ch. D, born 24.11.88, Misbourne Valdorki–Perrytree Sweet Dream. Br/owner, Mrs J. Rowland.

LYNWATER LITTLE OWL, Sh. Ch. B, born 1.5.88, Sh. Ch. Cleavehill Pot of Gold–Sh. Ch. Lynwater Tawny Owl. Br, Miss F. Wormell. Owner, Mrs E. Maclean.

JINESSKA GOLDEN PROSPECT FOR MANCHELA, Sh. Ch. D, born 28.9.89, Sh. Ch. Judika Titan–Cintillia Golden Rhythm. Br, Miss J. King. Owner, Mr M. J. Masters.

CANYONN CELESTE, Sh. Ch. B, born 13.5.91, Sh. Ch. Canyonn Carbon Copy–Sh. Ch. Canyonn Carolina Moon. Br/owner, Mrs S. Young.

LUJESA FIORE DORATO, Sh. Ch. B, born 7.7.90, Sh. Ch. Kells Clannad–Perrytree Queen of the Night. Brs/owners, Misses A. and S. Kettle.

ALLIES CHOICE, Sh. Ch., Irish Sh. Ch. D, born 24.5.90, Danymeade Hawthorn–Shaggy Girl. Br, Mrs P. Steward. Owners, Mr and Mrs J. H. Yardley.

QUETTADENE DISCRETION, Sh. Ch. D, born 13.5.91, Sh. Ch. Perrytree The Dreamer–Sh. Ch. Quettadene Modesty.

ASQUANNE'S GOLDFINGA, Sh. Ch. D, born 2.9.92, Sh. Ch. Kells Clannad–Sh. Ch. Asquanne's Ghia. Brs/owners, Mr and Mrs A. Webster.

Appendix

BRITISH BREED CLUBS

HAMPSHIRE & SUSSEX COCKER SPANIEL CLUB
Street Meadow, South
Warnborough,Basingstoke, Hants
RG25 1RD
Tel: 01256- 862747

HOME COUNTIES COCKER CLUB
Mrs S. Sadler, Rob Rosa,
Lower Road, Hockley,
Essex Tel: 01702-201966

COCKER SPANIEL CLUB OF LANCASHIRE
Mrs H. Ladanowski, Yew
Tree Farm, Norton,
Runcorn, Cheshire
WA7 2HUTel: 01928-714613

LONDON COCKER SPANIEL SOCIETY
Mr R.W. Crisp,
192 Westmoreland Avenue,
Limbury, Luton, Beds,
LU3 2PU Tel: 01582-508088

MIDLAND COCKER SPANIEL CLUB
Mr R.M.A. Pain, 57 New Inns Lane, Rubery, Birmingham,
B45 9TS
Tel: 0121-453-3215

NORTH OF IRELAND COCKER SPANIEL CLUB
Mr J. McDowell, 6 Knockagh Heights,Carrickfergus, N.
Ireland
BT38 8QZ
Tel: 01960 367659

**NORTH OF ENGLAND COCKER SPANIEL
ASSOCIATION**   Mrs J. Hill, 2 Park Avenue, Timperley,
Cheshire.
Tel: 0161 962 5278

**NORTH MIDLANDS & EASTERN COUNTIES
COCKER SPANIEL CLUB**
Mrs J. Pretty, Newlands Cottage, Stubby Lane, Marchington,
Uttoxeter, Staffs Tel: 01283 820867

NORTH WALES COCKER SPANIEL CLUB
Miss A. Hughes, 7 Ffordd Derwen, Rhyl, Clwyd, N Wales.
Tel: 01745 353715

PARTICOLOURED COCKER SPANIEL CLUB
Mrs D. Young, Bankside, Hollington, Ashbourne, Derbyshire
DE6 3GA Tel: 01335-60553

RED & GOLDEN COCKER SPANIEL CLUB
Acting Secretary: Miss S.Kettle, Marvay, Southend Road,
Corringham, Essex SS17 9ET
Tel: 01268 554619

**ROTHERHAM & DISTRICT COCKER SPANIEL
CLUB**
Mr A. Currey, 6 Mayfield Drive, Brayton, Selby Yorkshire
YO8 9JZ Tel: 01757-708105

COCKER SPANIEL CLUB OF SCOTLAND
Mrs A. Barnett, 140 Silvertonhill Avenue, Hamilton, ML3
7PA
Tel: 016948-428764

**SOUTH WALES & MONMOUTHSHIRE COCKER
SPANIEL CLUB**
Mrs J. Craig, 22 New Road, Ynysmeudwy, Pontardawe,
Swansea SA8 4PJ Tel: 01792 864402

ULSTER COCKER SPANIEL CLUB
Acting Secretary: Miss H. Crossan, 86 Downshire Road,
Holywood, Co. Down

WEST OF ENGLAND COCKER SPANIEL CLUB
Mr D. Shapland, The Old Post Office, Latton,Swindon, Wilts
Tel: 01793-75112

YORKSHIRE COCKER SPANIEL
Mr D. Shields,
Mcadowfields, 40 Thornton Road, Pickering, N.Yorkshire
YO18 7HZ
Tel: 01751-72641

COCKER SPANIELS BREEDERS DIRECTORY

WALES
CAEFARDRE
Mrs Ruth Clarke, Glandwr Close, Pandy, Abergavenny, Gwent NP7 8DW.
Tel: 01873 890602
Puppies Occasionally for Sale.

NORTH EAST
CLEAVEHILL
Mrs J. M. Taylor, Cleaves Lodge, Streetlam, Northallerton, N. Yorks DL7 0AJ.
Tel: 01325 378730
Dogs at Stud/Puppies Occasionally for Sale.

WEST MIDLANDS
CANIGOU
Mrs P. L. Bentley, The Firs, Somerwood, Rodington, Shrewsbury SY4 4RF.
Tel: 01952 770447
Dogs at Stud/Puppies Occasionally for Sale.

QUETTADENE
Mrs Penny Lester, Quettadene, Lichfield Road, Sandhills, Walsall Wood, West Midlands WS9 9PE.
Tel: 01543 373293
Dogs at Stud/Puppies Occasionally for Sale/Boarding Facilities Available.

EAST MIDLANDS
ASQUANNE
Mr & Mrs A. Webster, The White House, Breedol Brand, Osgathorpe, Leics. LE12 9ST
Tel: 01530 223570
Dogs at Stud/Puppies Occasionally for Sale/Boarding Facilities Available.

SOUTH WEST
PIPSMORE
Mrs J. A. Holley, Ivy Farm Cottage, West Yatton Keynell, Chippenham, Wilts. SN14 7EW.
Tel: 01249 782804
Dogs at Stud/Puppies Occasionally for Sale.

EAST ANGLIA
SPROGMORE
Mrs Anne Moore, Sprogmore Kennels, Alresford, Colchester, Essex CO7 8AP.
Tel: 01206 825781
Dogs at Stud/Puppies Occasionally for Sale/Boarding Facilities Available.

LONDON & HOME COUNTIES
KELLS
Mrs Lesley Gilmour-Wood, Kells Cottage, 84a Hampton Road, Twickenham, Middx. TW2 5QS.
Tel: 0181 894 0342
Dogs at Stud/Puppies Occasionally for Sale.

OF WARE and FALCONERS
Mrs Jennifer Lloyd Carey, 23 Iver Lane, Iver, Bucks SL0 9LH.
Tel: 01753 651617
Dogs at Stud/Puppies Occasionally for Sale.

CASSOM

SH. CH. CASSOM
APRIL SKY

Owned and bred by:
SARAH AMOS-JONES
CARLTON HALL
EAST CARLTON
YEADON
Nr LEEDS LS19 7BG

Tel: 0113 2509105

Puppies occasionally for sale

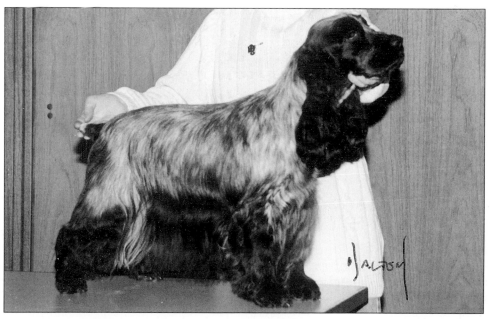